Shakespeare and Reception Theory

ARDEN SHAKESPEARE AND THEORY

Series Editor: Evelyn Gajowski

AVAILABLE TITLES

Shakespeare and Cultural Materialist Theory, Christopher Marlow
Shakespeare and Economic Theory, David Hawkes
Shakespeare and Ecocritical Theory, Gabriel Egan
Shakespeare and Ecofeminist Theory, Rebecca Laroche and Jennifer Munroe
Shakespeare and Feminist Theory, Marianne Novy
Shakespeare and New Historicist Theory, Neema Parvini
Shakespeare and Postcolonial Theory, Jyotsna G. Singh
Shakespeare and Posthumanist Theory, Karen Raber
Shakespeare and Psychoanalytic Theory, Carolyn Brown
Shakespeare and Queer Theory, Melissa E. Sanchez

FORTHCOMING TITLES

Shakespeare and Adaptation Theory, Sujata Iyengar
Shakespeare and Performance Theory, David McCandles
Shakespeare and Presentist Theory, Evelyn Gajowski
Shakespeare and Legal Theory, Karen J. Cunningham
Shakespeare and Race Theory, Arthur L. Little, Jr.
Shakespeare and Textual Theory, Suzanne Gossett

Shakespeare and Reception Theory

Nigel Wood

THE ARDEN SHAKESPEARE
LONDON • NEW YORK • OXFORD • NEW DELHI • SYDNEY

THE ARDEN SHAKESPEARE
Bloomsbury Publishing Plc
50 Bedford Square, London, WC1B 3DP, UK
1385 Broadway, New York, NY 10018, USA
29 Earlsfort Terrace, Dublin 2, Ireland

BLOOMSBURY, THE ARDEN SHAKESPEARE and the Arden Shakespeare logo are trademarks of Bloomsbury Publishing Plc

First published in Great Britain 2020
This paperback edition published in 2022

Copyright © Nigel Wood, 2020

Nigel Wood has asserted his right under the Copyright, Designs and Patents Act, 1988, to be identified as the author of this work.

For legal purposes the Acknowledgements on p. xii constitute an extension of this copyright page.

Series design by Sutchinda Rangsi Thompson
Cover image © Brainmaster / Getty Images

All rights reserved. No part of this publication may be reproduced or transmitted in any form or by any means, electronic or mechanical, including photocopying, recording, or any information storage or retrieval system, without prior permission in writing from the publishers.

Bloomsbury Publishing Plc does not have any control over, or responsibility for, any third-party websites referred to or in this book. All internet addresses given in this book were correct at the time of going to press. The author and publisher regret any inconvenience caused if addresses have changed or sites have ceased to exist, but can accept no responsibility for any such changes.

A catalogue record for this book is available from the British Library.

A catalog record for this book is available from the Library of Congress.

ISBN:	HB:	978-1-3501-1210-0
	PB:	978-1-3502-0090-6
	ePDF:	978-1-3501-1212-4
	eBook:	978-1-3501-1211-7

Series: Shakespeare and Theory

Typeset by RefineCatch Limited, Bungay, Suffolk

To find out more about our authors and books visit www.bloomsbury.com and sign up for our newsletters.

To Dominic, Isabelle and Milo

CONTENTS

Series Editor's Preface ix
Acknowledgements xii

Introduction 1

1 First Principles 13

2 The Role of the Spectator and Reader 29

3 Literary Communities and Affective Experience 63

4 The Resistant Reader 91

5 Shakespeare and Public Responses 123

Conclusion 151

Appendix 163
Notes 165
References 173
Index 189

SERIES EDITOR'S PREFACE

'Asking questions about literary texts – that's literary criticism. Asking "Which questions shall we ask about literary texts?" – that's literary theory'. So goes my explanation of the current state of English studies, and Shakespeare studies, in my never-ending attempt to demystify, and simplify, theory for students in my classrooms. Another way to put it is that theory is a systematic account of the nature of literature, the act of writing and the act of reading.

One of the primary responsibilities of any academic discipline – whether in the natural sciences, the social sciences or the humanities – is to examine its methodologies and tools of analysis. Particularly at a time of great theoretical ferment, such as that which has characterized English studies, and Shakespeare studies, in recent years, it is incumbent upon scholars in a given discipline to provide such reflection and analysis. We all construct meanings in Shakespeare's texts and culture. Shouldering responsibility for our active role in constructing meanings in literary texts, moreover, constitutes a theoretical stance. To the extent that we examine our own critical premises and operations, that theoretical stance requires reflection on our part. It requires honesty, as well. It is thereby a fundamentally radical act. All critical analysis puts into practice a particular set of theoretical premises. Theory occurs from a particular standpoint. There is no critical practice that is somehow devoid of theory. There is no critical practice that is not implicated in theory. A common-sense, transparent encounter with any text is thereby impossible. Indeed, to the extent that theory requires us to question anew that with which we thought we were familiar, that which we thought we understood, theory constitutes a critique of common sense.

Since the advent of postmodernism, the discipline of English studies has undergone a seismic shift. The discipline of Shakespeare studies has been at the epicentre of this shift. Indeed, it has been Shakespeare scholars who have played a major role in several of the theoretical and critical developments (e.g. new historicism, cultural materialism, presentism) that have shaped the discipline of English studies in recent years. Yet a comprehensive scholarly analysis of these crucial developments has yet to be done, and is long overdue. As the first series to foreground analysis of contemporary theoretical developments in the discipline of Shakespeare studies, *Arden Shakespeare and Theory* aims to fill a yawning gap.

To the delight of some and the chagrin of others, since 1980 or so, theory has dominated Shakespeare studies. *Arden Shakespeare and Theory* focuses on the state of the art at the outset of the twenty-first century. For the first time, it provides a comprehensive analysis of the theoretical developments that are emerging at the present moment, as well as those that are dominant or residual in Shakespeare studies.

Each volume in the series aims to offer the reader the following components: to provide a clear definition of a particular theory; to explain its key concepts; to trace its major developments, theorists and critics; to perform a reading of a Shakespeare text; to elucidate a specific theory's intersection with or relationship to other theories; to situate it in the context of contemporary political, social and economic developments; to analyse its significance in Shakespeare studies; and to suggest resources for further investigation. Authors of individual volumes thereby attempt to strike a balance, bringing their unique expertise, experience and perspectives to bear upon particular theories while simultaneously fulfilling the common purpose of the series. Individual volumes in the Series are devoted to elucidating particular theoretical perspectives, such as adaptation, cultural materialism, ecocriticism, ecofeminism, economic theory, feminism, film theory, legal theory, new historicism, performance, postcoloniality, posthumanism, presentism, psychoanalysis, queer theory, race theory, reception, and textual theory.

Arden Shakespeare and Theory aims to enable scholars, teachers and students alike to define their own theoretical strategies and refine their own critical practices. And students have as much at stake in these theoretical and critical enterprises – in the reading and the writing practices that characterize our discipline – as do scholars and teachers. Janus-like, the series looks forward as well as backward, serving as an inspiration and a guide for new work in Shakespeare studies at the outset of the twenty-first century, on the one hand, and providing a retrospective analysis of the intellectual labour that has been accomplished in recent years, on the other.

To return to the beginning: what is at stake in our reading of literary texts? Once we come to understand the various ways in which theory resonates with not only Shakespeare's texts, and literary texts, but the so-called 'real' world – the world outside the world of the mind, the world outside the world of academia – then we come to understand that theory is capable of powerfully enriching not only our reading of Shakespeare's texts, and literary texts, but our lives.

* * *

I am indebted to David Avital, publisher at Bloomsbury Academic, who was instrumental in developing the idea of the *Arden Shakespeare and Theory* series. I am also grateful to Margaret Bartley and Mark Dudgeon, publishers for the Arden Shakespeare, for their guidance and support throughout the development of this series.

Evelyn Gajowski
Series Editor
University of Nevada, Las Vegas

ACKNOWLEDGEMENTS

Remembering the theatrical experiments of the final-year *Contemporary Shakespeare* students at Loughborough University, 2018/19, and the contributions of fellow Public Sphere investigators, Jeffrey S. Doty, Alison Findlay, Missa Gurnis, Michael Mangan, Stephen Purcell and Erin Sullivan.

Introduction

In the Royal Shakespeare Company's 1997–8 run of *Twelfth Night* (dir. Adrian Noble) at the Memorial Theatre in Stratford-upon-Avon, the most show-stopping moment might have been most unexpected for the cast. Sir Andrew's plaintive, 'I am a great eater of beef, and I believe that does harm to my wit' (1.3.84–5)[1] was greeted with prolonged and loud laughter and, on some nights, applause. As the season progressed, John Quayle, as Sir Andrew, acknowledged a sort of defeat (or victory) by anticipating the response and regularly gazed out into the dark with a meaningful stare, and held the pose until the hiatus in the action had ceased. Not in itself particularly witty, one had to understand the date of utterance of the line, not resort to an early modern explanation. While there is one – a pervasive medical theory that beef ingestion did indeed slow the brain (see Thersites' jibe at Ajax as a 'beef-witted lord' in *Troilus and Cressida* (2.1.13)), the root cause derived from a gathering storm in 1990s Britain surrounding the pernicious tragedy of an apparently unstoppable epidemic known popularly as Mad Cow Disease (or, more technically, bovine spongiform encephalopathy). As recently as March 1996, the British government had confirmed that the condition could be transmitted to humans; exports were banned and whole herds burnt. The amusement was a recognition that phrases could attract 'apt' meanings anachronistically, and the laughter (unfortunately the loudest in the performances I saw) was derived from what the public brought to the text rather than what they registered as 'in' the text – originally and directly. This is not just a matter of ontology – how *Twelfth Night* may now be said to exist – but rather one as true of any original source: its address to any anticipated audience depends on the local and transitory as well as what remains for posterity. One might segregate performance as only contingent upon any playtext, but it does stem from connotations and a relationship to spectators that can be embedded in its verbal existence originally, even if only actuated at a later date due to inevitably unforeseen factors. Its relevance stems from its reminder that any use of context is largely a matter of guess and hunch, the catching of the transitory, of signifiers on the wing.

This is to recognize the experiences of a sufficiently literate audience as of paramount significance – and whether the text catered for them principally. Alternatively, one's approach to the verbal texture of any drama should allow for radical surprise, the provision of shock and less rehearsed effects that elude immediate categorization. It is therefore one qualitative test of how any playtext survives that its potential for public performance alters and prompts re-formed alliances with new audiences. That is why our own senses of 'audience' and/or 'play' need analysis as the content of these terms has recently undergone a material shift into electronic and hidden forms of manipulation, where complexes of non-literary as well as theatrical effects supply implicit conventions of seeing and participation. Playtexts are also distinctive records of intention. Writers can attempt to shackle future interpretation by explicit stage directions or, more indirectly, by lengthy introductions to printed forms of the text. In Shakespeare's case, neither of these signs of ownership are evident. Far from being a weakness, this is a licence for liberal and creative appropriation.

This is not, however, a modern phenomenon. The staple ingredient of how drama survives is verbal, but that opens rather than closes interpretive options. For Shakespeare's first audiences, certain keywords or phrases were heard – and thus understood – in subtly modified ways in the playhouse and therefore signified via distinctive cognitive processes. This normally lies outside the brief for even the minutest investigations that textual editors regard as their task. We expect the annotation in the best editions to perform the task of restoring meaning to words or phrases that had impact in first performances, yet this recovery work – piecemeal and inevitably localized – rarely takes full account of the relay of semes that gather force in live performance and that assume crucial significance for particular audiences.

Attending a Shakespeare in the Park open-air performance of *Henry IV, Part 1* at the Delacorte Theater (July 1981) in Central Park (New York), Falstaff – as per script – seemed to be a fatality of war following the stage direction: 'He [Douglas] fighteth with Sir John who falls down as if he were dead' (5.4.75). The mode of the skirmish was realistic, involving a pained final exhalation from Kenneth McMillan as Falstaff that extracted a sigh of regret from those around me. I was proof against such instincts because I well knew that Falstaff was to survive, yet perhaps I lost something with that knowledge, for at the point when Hal exits – after a touching elegy on 'poor Jack' (5.4.102) – the mood is shattered with his 'resurrection' at 5.4.110; the crowd cheered and whooped. The witty scoundrel was to entertain us for a little longer, but I was proof against such impulsive immersion because I had seen the gesture before and had taught the text. My approach was destined to be analytic first and participatory later. Indeed, one could argue that such participation was now impossible for me, and my involvement could never be at one with those witnessing the scene for the first time. Looking back at that moment, I found that a series of associated issues were presented to me: if we can accept that any 'first-night' audience would encounter Falstaff's 'death' moment-by-moment and therefore would have been as pleasantly surprised as the spectators, then I would have to 'unlearn' much of my knowledge about the dramatic action in order to recapture some of that surprise. As a route back to any anticipated strategy on Shakespeare's behalf, the quality of that emotional release would have to be registered at some level and its attendant reflection upon how complex our perspective on the character could be, for Falstaff is a 'counterfeit' but only in one sense, as he notes that, on a material plane, 'to die is to be a counterfeit' (5.4.114–15). The lifeless Hotspur, who had so fervently encouraged us to believe in the sanctity of honour and chivalry when alive, portrays a possible death of those great abstract nouns. Falstaff survives (and we want him to), and perhaps there is a wry smile when he uses the corpse as a stage prop in taking it on his back (*s.d.*, 5.4.128) in a desperate attempt to verify his own fake valour before Hal and Lancaster. On the other hand, our co-option as Falstaff supporters carries with it an obligation to realize just what it is that we are countenancing: values that confirm fakery and that might allow us to regard honourable behaviour as outmoded and even foolish: 'Nothing confutes me but eyes, and nobody sees me' (5.4.124–5).

The relevance of these two anecdotes is that they involve reactions to drama and – even more precisely – to responses to Shakespearean drama. There are a cluster of questions that could be posed when reflecting on these episodes. First, the delight in an anachronistic – and therefore perhaps inappropriate – reference in Aguecheek's fear about beef-eating was unshunnable and instinctive. As such, it could be classed as an authentic experience, even if not one that was likely to have been a pervasive early modern one. How that 1990s audience might have encountered *Twelfth Night* then stands equivalent to an enquiry as to how any original spectators might have encountered the performance: which might help us to establish how we should view and evaluate the text? What we encounter before too long is the need to explain the process of reception – how the action is comprehended and appreciated. The trigger for such laughter might indeed have been actuated by the text, but any explanation as to how it came to life could only partially be explained by quotation, in that it was what was brought to the event by the spectators that provided the key.

As a parable of how drama works, this episode is valid on two counts: principally, it draws attention to what was done with the words both by the acting company and how they were received by its audience on the way to producing meaning on the one hand and on the other to assessing their theatrical power. Secondarily, though, this 'sense' arrives out of a process of negotiation with the text. Any laugh may appear to be instinctive, but it does not follow that it is purely automatic in causation. Any reference to the ingestion of beef in the twenty-first century or earlier in the 1950s, say, would have flown by, but it is possible that other flashpoints would emerge at that time to detain or attract audience attention. The marking of dramatic dissonance, say, or confirmation, or of discomfort or shock, is never constant throughout history either in terms of its intensity or often in terms of its very appearance. The wish to identify some stability in what has been transmitted to us in Shakespeare's words is thwarted by the rediscovery in performance of semantic nuances that may lie outside the verbal lexicon.

It is not a large step to the Delacorte Theater instance: the release of tension or shock of the unexpected once Falstaff revives is greatest if this is the first time we sense it. The experienced Shakespearean would not be able to share in these reactions. Additionally, there is a permission allowed an audience in most open-air performances to be voluble in one's reaction; indeed the tradition at the Delacorte, while most certainly not inviting uncritical estimates, is that an audience is part of the action, and the director on that night, Des McAnuff, was quite properly clearly alert to that.

Reception theory is key to a theatrical understanding of how drama's effects might be registered. It is, therefore, basic to any comprehension of the meanings that are carried and promoted in performance. The term 'theatrical' attracts a cluster of semantic nuances that will be explored in this volume, as will the term 'dramatic', and it is essential that some initial mapping of these terms is attempted. It is also undertaken with a recognition that much investigation of artistic effect is not directly focused on the dramatic event; the precision involved in coming to terms (literally) with how drama specifically communicates is a vital issue and is usually attempted by reference to performance cognition. Running parallel to this, there is plentiful involvement in assessing the aesthetics of how readers trace meanings and this is rarely applied to a purely theatrical environment. Any attempt to combine these two approaches has to judge where some priorities true of reading might be less appropriate to an assessment of how it contributes to an awareness of a playtext's potential.

Ultimately, what we should remember about both of these anecdotes is that they commemorate an event, the shock that is memorable and the transgression that is meaningful. Literary as well as theatrical history can be a simple chronology, an account of temporal succession, yet that is not a rationale for new meanings that might supplant or supplement past ones. Indeed, how any meaning-event emerges from the moment is a much more complex affair, because values and their significance cannot be insulated from contingency. When we respond in our reading or spectating, can we sift the apparently 'accidental' from the thematic and strategic? In the moment, we react and do so without an immediate concern with posterity, tradition or even authorial intention. This is especially the case where theatre is the test bed; an audience's full-throated affirmation or rapt silence is the product of complex factors.

The aim of this study is to embrace and exemplify the variety of studies focused on how meaning is achieved (hermeneutics) and also how artistic significance might be projected quite separately from more pragmatic means of communication (aesthetics). Inevitably, this will be attempted as far as Shakespearean examples are concerned with few precedents, even if there have been several theoretical readings of audience response and narrative cognition. Often this is perceived as conceptual weakness in that a purely subjective emotion evades easy categorization and analysis, but studies of response are as much an exploration of what might seem individual and imaginatively escapist as it is of how dramatic structures might function and – sociologically speaking – how audiences might, pre-emptively, be coerced into prescribed witness.

It is dazzling to survey the excellent and provocative contributions to just how – specifically – drama might communicate, challenge and entertain us. I have to be selective and, inevitably, this discloses my own bias, but I proceed from a basic reflection on drama in general: the imitation of actions in a more or less interdependent framework is given weight once we note the theatrical context. For example, nowadays, it is customary to book tickets and willingly enter this or that space to view such imitations due to any number of generic motives that condition our expectations and thus the spectrum of potential meanings. Moreover, there are distinctions worth our attention as to whether we enter a space hallowed by a need to appreciate the most skilled dramatic art in a venerable auditorium – at Stratford-upon-Avon, say, or Stratford, Ontario – or some back room in a public house or bar during a Fringe festival or on the street or in the open air, where the cultural imperatives are more faintly in play. The cultural icon that is 'Shakespeare' is now inescapable and his scripts now carry their own freight; to some, this is an opportunity to subvert and disconcert, and to others it could be a deadening weight that closes down options for authentic drama.

In attempting to co-opt reception theories towards an enhanced understanding of Shakespearean texts, I am aware that several of my chosen writers do not directly address dramatic values in their writings, yet the search for hermeneutic validity and variety exceeds any analysis of the precise factors we commonly associate with performance. The opening chapter provides a survey of some ideas associated with the most influential theorists of response and also those who have contributed to more recent assumptions about theatrical effect. Chapter 2 aims to grasp the significance of addressing what occurs when we interact with performance. To this end, it will start by considering the theories of Hans Robert Jauss,

Wolfgang Iser and Umberto Eco. Although different in their emphases, these approaches have two issues in common: (a) can we explain how one epoch can have a very specific link with a text and another produce quite an alternative relationship with it?, and (b) how functional might an aesthetic experience be in the assembling of meanings, either as a result of some implied authorial intention or as a symptom of ideological or other epistemological shifts? The common reference point is *Antony and Cleopatra*.

Chapter 3 is more behavioural in its investigations of the 'dynamics of literary response' – to borrow Norman Holland's phrase. For Holland, there is always an unacknowledged transference of what appear to be personal needs or assumptions about identity onto any text we read or see, leading to the possibility of a 'resymbolization', as David Bleich has it, of these preoccupations in our recognition of the literary or dramatic event. However, reading behaviours are culturally conditioned in some part by the recognition of interpretive solidarity, and, as Stanley Fish terms it, we are hailed by 'interpretive communities', or, as Jonathan Culler finds, acquired 'competences' that structure our reading and spectating habits. This is illustrated with reference to *A Midsummer Night's Dream*.

What happens when the sense of where we might orientate ourselves more comfortably no longer holds good? In Chapter 4, looking in detail at *The Taming of the Shrew*, *Coriolanus*, *The Merchant of Venice* and *The Tempest*, I look at strategies of resistance where we might refuse the co-option of a performance text. At its most extreme, the process becomes one of identifying – and then remapping new emphases – our training in spectating or reading. As Judith Fetterley terms it (in her case where a female reader is concerned), some scripts co-opt us 'in an experience from which [one] is explicitly excluded' and where our role is defined 'in opposition' to us. Consequently, one is minded to 'identify against [oneself]' (Fetterley 1978: xii). How can we accomplish that? Perhaps one course might be to refuse the need to evaluate in a context of 'masterpiece theatre', as Jane Tompkins demonstrates in the light of her cold view of Hawthorne's reputation. If we do not go in search of how the classics determine our sense of value, then we recast a sense of the canon and thus of significant aesthetics (Tompkins 2001: 133–54). This extends outside normal disciplinary parameters and embraces more fundamental issues of canon formation. For John Frow, this move

> involves deciding that, rather than engaging in a discourse of value, calculating the relative worth of this text against that text according to some impossibly universal criterion of value, the job of the critic is rather to analyse the social relations of value themselves: to analyse the discourses of value, the socially situated frameworks of valuation from which value judgements are generated by readers [or we might add, spectators].
>
> FROW 2001: 296

Far from peripheral, how a Jewish viewer might truly regard *The Merchant of Venice* or how a spectator of colour engage with *The Tempest* becomes far more pivotal for all acts of spectating or playing.

In the last chapter, I dwell on how far contextual studies of Shakespearean texts might or should guide us in analysing their performance with reference to aspects of Jürgen Habermas's ideas of how our motives and behaviour are affected when we sense we are in a 'public sphere'. The issue is one of assessing differences in 'private' and 'public' significations both in Shakespeare's society as well as our own. In the recent studies by Balme and Doty, there is recorded a sense that performing is not confined to specific theatres at appointed times and seasons but rather how this was woven into the fabric of so much social interaction. Might the early modern senses of 'playing' or 'ceremony' survive to guide us in our own lexicon? By exploring the rituals embedded in both *Henry V* and *Hamlet* I attempt to provide an account of how both plays reach out to and construct their audiences, and also how our own theatre going should be conscious of how both narratives might now be regarded in our own 'public sphere' possibilities.

This study employs several theoretical templates, but I hope it coheres around the focus on diachronies of both the 'theatre' and 'drama' as an art form. Inevitably, it will involve reflections on the status of aesthetics and the 'semiotics of theatrical performance', as Umberto Eco has it, where (in the most effective drama) we do not maintain a scepticism that what we see on stage is fabricated. A cluster of trees on stage might be the Forest of Arden, a wood near Athens or Birnam Wood; they cannot be – in the most literal sense – merely trees in the most severe botanical sense. How they are framed and set to work involves subtly differentiated expectations and these specimens painted on a backdrop perhaps are not 'real' but they are no simple renditions of any copse we might see when out walking. From this perspective, they are signs of signs that call to mind the 'real' for purposes quite different from verisimilitude. These stage trees thereby call forth a cluster of associations: of uncourtly pastoral simplicity (harsh, yet redemptive), of magical possibilities beyond the normal or the encroachment of Fate and the fulfilment of perhaps diabolic prophecy (see Eco 1977: 107–17). We are the interpreters and decoders of these signs, yet as the example of Andrew Aguecheek's fear of beef-eating in 1997 might illustrate, these signs are not universal; they are susceptible to modernization and expansion. We should embrace the creativity of diversity by searching for the authenticity of what we experience. For Norman Holland, certain performances invite us to recognize 'identity themes', sites of immersion or recognition that take us out of ourselves. Thus, 'we work out through the text our own characteristic patterns of desire and adaptation. We interact with the work, making it part of our own psychic economy and making ourselves part of the literary work – as we interpret it' (Holland 1980: 124).

To achieve this depth of analysis where performance is concerned, it is also advantageous to consider how the oral differs from the written. As Walter J. Ong has advised us, writing structures consciousness as 'print encourages a sense of closure, a sense that what is found in a text has been finalized, has reached a state of completion'. In addition, it depicts – or has the capacity so to do – 'more tightly closed verbal art forms' that stand distinct from an oral contact that brings into play other priorities (Ong 1982: 132, 133). It is therefore a basic task to investigate just what alternative forms of cognition are available to us in the auditorium.

When we congregate to see and hear a play, there is an instructive question to pose: 'when does the performance start?' Has it already commenced via advance publicity, or our knowledge of the play in question? These are central to any act of interpretation, because the search for detailed answers brings into play sociologies of playgoing that unearth the cultural status of such an activity and, in turn, offer templates of anticipation against which we acquiesce or from which we are asked to stand distinct. The acting brings into being the script of the play, yet the deterministic qualities of what we take to be Shakespeare's thoughts cannot survive intact in the process of active spectating, no matter how traditional we try to render it. The meanings will not stay still. It is in this sense that we both 'perform' our roles as audience members and yet are open to the 'performative' occasion itself, where the physical rendition calls into being meanings, emotions and objects that irreducibly evade easy paraphrase. Performances are often 'performative' in the way that speech act theory has it, derived from J. L. Austin's distinction between 'constative' utterances – which can be confirmed as meaningful by a correspondence with tangible reality – and 'performative' utterances that accomplish something in the very fact of expression, such as promising, taking an oath, or saying 'I do' in the wedding ceremony. Austin's underlying project was to bypass issues of intention and to analyse statements more by their linguistic structure, to discover their 'illocutionary' force, the net result in cognitive terms of any linguistic formulation. The problem remains, however, as to how to identify any 'nonserious' or ironic or fictive use of language. The actor portraying Hamlet at any one point, one hopes, never contemplates suicide or thinks of the world as a prison.

Austin himself introduces a theatrical instance when discussing the limits of performative utterance:

> A performative utterance will be ... *in a peculiar way* hollow or void if said by an actor on the stage or introduced in a poem, or spoken in a soliloquy. This applies in a similar manner to any and every utterance – a sea-change in special circumstances. Language in such circumstances is in special ways – intelligibly – used not seriously, but in ways *parasitic* upon its normal use – ways which fall under the doctrine of the *etiolations* of language ... Our performative utterances, felicitous or not, are to be understood as issued in ordinary circumstances.
>
> AUSTIN 1975: 21–2

The concept that a theatrical utterance cannot be, by this yardstick, *serious* is judged by Austin according to a template of 'ordinary circumstances', where 'intelligibility' is the goal derived from 'constative' aims. There is the hope that by concentrating on response and the 'special circumstances' of drama, one might find that its statements are deeply serious.

1

First Principles

Before we consider more recent reception theories, it would be as well to glance at some formative ideas that have shaped both hermeneutic and aesthetic thought. Hermeneutic studies are concerned with how we might interpret external data, both textual and non-textual, clearly and accurately, and aesthetics with how we might register the experiences derived principally from art. In several respects, there is considerable overlap. There are at least four main issues that have engaged reception theorists:

1. Are the distinctive *artistic* elements that encourage certain types of viewing and reading identifiable as, ultimately, residing in the literary/dramatic work; or
2. Is the crucial factor a psychological one, manifest only through isolating an awareness of one's impulses and subjectivity, thereby leading to conclusions as to how we read or spectate?
3. To what extent is it valuable to study past reactions to literary artefacts, wherein we focus on some sense of the implications shared with past audiences and which may now elude us? And finally,
4. Is it possible to regard some works in manufactured and willed ways that are perhaps more politically or relevant aside from any first, instinctive, reaction? How might we alter or reject earlier (and less valuable)

pleasures or judgements in the service of what we might take, on reflection, as a higher good?

Overall, the aim of these critical emphases, where Shakespeare's plays are concerned, is to apply relevant criteria to their interpretation and evaluation, and that entails an exploration of how they might have been constructed with a likely audience in mind – with a focus on the conventions of spectating and creating that obtained at the time of first performance – but also how these words and gestures reached out to spectator reaction and experience. This is only part of the agenda, however, as the theoretical considerations of how meaning is achieved in the theatre conditions an awareness of how Shakespeare might now be understood in the deepest and most radical of senses.

The move to estimate what happens when we make sense of art – its phenomenology – is often credited to Edmund Husserl, whose major works analyse how we express feelings and therefore ideas caused by external events. Instead of reaching out to such experiential data and attempting to identify a common cause of root experiences therefrom, Husserl wanted to get at the authenticity of how we personally and truly experience. In his two-volume *Logical Investigations* (1900/1) and then refined in his *Ideas* (1913; Husserl 1982), he inaugurates studies into how much we are often prey to what he calls a 'natural attitude' wherein we experience what we are supposed to and what would be comfortable so to do: a stance 'in which we all live and from which we start when we bring about the philosophical transformation of our viewpoint'. The world of 'pre-given things' (*Vorfindlichkeiten*) is understood as obvious (Husserl 2006: 2). Back in 1891, and in his *Philosophy of Arithmetic,* Husserl had shown an early interest in the precognitive bases that underlay computation – its function as fact and how it satisfies certain emotional as well as practical requirements; indeed, the practical follows from aims that satisfy in some way. The most accessible illustration could be the motivation behind 'To prove' in any basic scientific experiment – which is apt to hide – while indicating – the need to experiment in this area in the first place.

The self, anchored by a notion of oneself as 'I', is not quite the sum of the varied experiences and intuitions that result from life – through our body and as a result of how we are situated temporally and often spatially. Art allows us to reach beyond this individual subjectivity because we are called upon to experience another 'I' and, assuming that we have the 'empathy' to travel with that other self, it is as if we intuit a wider arena of knowledge and emotion than that we started with. Traversing along a road in sight of a mountain, say, what we see at one point might lead us to predict what would be visible, but is at this moment out of our sight. If we took the trouble to take a full circuit of the mountain, then our knowledge of what is named on a map as the eminence would be fuller and it might well instal itself in our memory as an experience. Normality is promoted by cartography (or in the linguistic world, a dictionary or formal word-system), a 'lifeworld', yet such knowledge is not what Husserl most concerns himself with (Husserl 2006: 5–8).

Subsequent thinkers have gained most from what Husserl terms a 'transcendental phenomenology': although we have to start with the subjective in order to gain the greatest and most direct access to lived experience, such instances are often momentary and sometimes just pass us by. The 'philosophical' attitude, however, involves us in transcending (or thinking beyond) that moment with the knowledge that the apparent purity of such impulses is in fact also a result of memory and situation. Gradually accumulating, the associations that have gathered around, for example, *Macbeth*, need to be 'bracketed off' from the particular performance of the play we are now witnessing. Certain recurrent traits that we acknowledge as the play so named form a kind of 'horizon-consciousness' that both aid comprehensibility – but might also retard it if we pigeonhole new experiences too rigidly. It is thus the case that the witches that commence the play may or may not be the principal source of Macbeth's tragic flaw; the same issue could be derived from how Lady Macbeth is allowed to be the fall-girl to account for and so excuse her husband's evil. Is it the case that we reject a particular reading of the action because it seems to us not to 'fit' – and then we leave it at that? To emerge from our inherited 'horizon-consciousness' we have to undergo a form of 'phenomenological reduction' whereby we bring to our consciousness this necessary division of the residual baggage from the past or tradition (also perhaps advertising or how we have been educated) from the here and now.[1]

The emphasis Husserl introduces into the work of interpretation is that it is worth exploring a distinction between meaning and object. In art, especially, the artwork exists as it is perceived, and as it is understood as an 'intentional object', the product of another consciousness.[2] Thus, we cannot know for sure what Shakespeare may have consciously intended; even if authors left behind plentiful evidence of their ideas through introductions, letters or journals, the work is apt to exceed a prosaic account. By an 'intentional object', Husserl has a notion of the interpreter obliged to work towards a model of eventual coherence. We might pause here to reflect upon this assumption: do writers have a developed consciousness of how deeply felt metaphors or other figures add up? Should they? This may be an insistent question where theatre is concerned in that nailing down a 'message' is not often regarded as the highest aesthetic and dramatic value. We do, though, have before us the complex task of accounting for how artefacts communicate and this entails an avoidance of the simplification in paraphrase. In the work of Hans-Georg Gadamer and Roman Ingarden, this mode of enquiry involves a negotiation between the work and interpreter. For Gadamer, in studies such as *Truth and Method* (1960; English editions: 1st: 1975, 2nd: 1989), 'method' is really self-fulfilling, a means to standardize according to prior assumptions in order to achieve a neatness directed by such priorities: this is to be distinguished from 'truth', our 'being-in-the world', which, crucially, is neither equivalent to scientific accuracy or consistency nor possesses a pragmatic function. The attractiveness of such a practical focus is that it allows for variable approaches given different contexts. It also situates understanding as the result of dialogue and a modification of any initial perspectives by which we might develop others' perceptions (that ideally become shared). In this, our improved approach to literature becomes a form of moral knowledge. Unlike a scientific language, literary expression is best instanced as a form of self-expression and a reaction to this is not an assessment of its practicality but rather an evaluation of how it bears upon everyday life and thus sensation. It is an activity, not an achievement of stasis and finite knowledge. Inevitably, in this social (and sociable) arena, the goal is to embrace a 'performative interpretation' wherein the self and one's starting preferences are not to be unreflectively set aside but, alternatively, put to work, challenged – and rendered more complex – in a form of conversation or dialectic with congenial others. Drama is no pure form in that it is left to performance conventions to attempt to interpret for spectators. Yet, however much there may be 'normative' assumptions in play (theatrical space, director's decisions in line with regular expectations), there is still an opening for what Gadamer calls 'cognitive' perception where we break through traditional filters and reach a more individualistic focus (see Gadamer 2014: 320–2). This means ultimately that the elements of staging are merely various means to a more reflective end. Persistently, Gadamer is drawn to the theatre to provide test cases: 'The performance of a play, like that of a ritual, cannot be simply detached from the play itself, as if it were something that is not part of its essential being, but is as subjective and fluid as the aesthetic experiences in which it is experienced' (Gadamer 2014: 120). Unexpectedly perhaps, Gadamer goes out of his way to collapse the world of representation (for example, actors or stage designers) into the world of its reception: we judge how *well* the performance succeeds by having an initial grasp of the text itself. Nothing can come of nothing. We then are well placed to judge its practical value upon our life choices and perceptions. There has to be some dislocation between the possible fandom of witnessing the playing out of a star system on stage or a ritual whereby our more traditional selves are confirmed, on the one hand, and, on the other, a more considered and holistic view (through aesthetic reflection) that permits a sense of challenge, even discomfort, that emerges from our contemplation of critical 'play'. The pun on 'play' ushers in a profound concentration of allied yet eventually divergent senses: of a staged representation, recreation, the actor's activity and latitude (in a technical sense of 'give', indicating the certain looseness of operation of a mechanism). In a game, while there may be agreed rules (without which the game would indeed cease to exist), charting quite how one exploits these in a specific realization is far from formulaic. Far from an extreme example of literature, a staged play is used by Gadamer to resemble the condition of all art (see Gadamer 2014: 121–30).

Moreover, just as any performance of a play is always situated spatially – in a particular theatre for a target audience – it is also inextricable from pre-existent conditions embedded in history. I cannot 'play' in my interpretation free of not only what I now sense but also how I came to recognize the 'truth' or accuracy in (in short, the value of) any work. We approach art relative to where we have now arrived in history – with our inherited ways of seeing or noticing. What is more, the clearest view of any object under scrutiny is more efficiently grasped once we 'play' with opinions to realize factors that are historically determined and perhaps free ourselves from them; we also need to break free from any egoistic adherence to 'what I believe', recognizing that, say, what we may take as authentic at age twenty may undergo radical change once we hit fifty, and that this alteration is not just a matter of maturation but temporal change in cultural terms.[3] The most memorable, and so valuable, experiences cannot always be captured and described easily, but Gadamer would prefer to see these, even if in a preliminary consideration, as inferred from the work: 'Thus it is not at all a question of a mere subjective variety of conceptions, but of the work's own possibilities of being that emerge as the work explicates itself, as it were, in the variety of its aspects' (Gadamer 2014: 122). In addition, there is as a consequence no sense involved of searching for a *correct* or *definitive* interpretation, because we should also sense that there cannot be – by definition – a 'fixed criterion' of value that is transhistorical (Gadamer 2014: 123).

We are thereby prey to the available 'horizon' through which we perceive and find matters comprehensible. Gadamer defines this term as 'a range of vision that includes everything that can be seen from a particular vantage point'. This is not just inescapable but also a condition that is enabling: we escape a perspective that is conditioned only to note what is nearest by looking beyond the immediate or obvious: 'similarly, working out the hermeneutical situation means acquiring the right horizon of inquiry for the questions evoked by the encounter with tradition' (Gadamer 2014: 313). This is why art is essential, for at its best it addresses the whole human being and, if we strive for a developed aesthetic and self-aware reflection, it promotes possibilities for change and a complex engagement with the processes of enquiry.

One of Husserl's students, Roman Ingarden worked on the invitation in his mentor's work to account for specifically *aesthetic* effects. How do we approach and interpret artefacts as distinct from other forms of communication? In two works, *The Literary Work of Art* (written 1926; 1st ed. in German, 1931; Ingarden 1973a) and *The Cognition of the Work of Art* (in German, 1968; Ingarden 1973b), he, however, does not stress an interpreter's power of transforming any object of her/his analysis in a realm completely independent of its cause. His hope was that, if we could enumerate the literary features of any text, we could literally come to terms with its more successful qualities and its overall value as art. Thus, he arrives at an identification of four separate zones: word sounds or phonetic effects (for example, melodies and rhythmic stress), units of meaning (relating to original semantic possibilities), schematized aspects (how references in the chosen text, such as characters or locations, are situated thematically) and representations. Ultimately, these components will compose an 'organic unity', even if the path to such a goal might be rather circuitous (Ingarden 1973a: 30, 33). Indeed, as we view or read, this awareness is usually beyond us. It is only by *reflection* (for Ingarden, a crucial step) that we can 'concretize' the work and come to an appreciation of its unitary existence. It is only by these means that debates of value can progress and points of real difference be isolated (Ingarden 1973a: 332–55). Furthermore, it is only by *demonstrating* artistic values that the work may be thoroughly understood. Such 'concretizations' are not perennial, though, as they may change via ensuing discussion or considering more mature experience in aesthetic cognition. The principle, on the other hand, would remain the same, and the worth of intricate compositions differentiated from merely consumerist fodder. Intuition is not missing from this approach; rather, it confronts a fully illustrated sense of how such a valuable work adds up. Ingarden, though, only allows drama into the literary ranks as a borderline case. The possibility for reflective analysis derives from a myriad of practical and material considerations that cannot always relate to any playtext in conventional ways. If, as he makes clear, this analysis can only fruitfully occur once we grasp a sense of the whole, a 'qualitative harmony in intuitive apprehension' that is composed of 'concepts . . . saturated with emotional elements' but which lead to 'strictly formulated judgements' (Ingarden 1973b: 210), then we minimize aspects of duration and the plasticity of representation wherein, performance by performance, there may be iconographic codes that are not directly inferred from the original text.

We do not reinvent any play once we review it subsequently. There is some demonstrable value in claiming that any performance is better than others, so there has to be a yardstick by which to substantiate such claims, an identifiable potential that gives rise to any number of serial experiences. Any written drama has a main text and what Ingarden calls a 'side' text, composed more or less directly from stage directions (in Shakespeare's case, these are often deduced from the main text's verbal content). One has to determine concretely in drama certain possibilities that are part of a series of alternatives realized immaterially while reflecting on any reading experience. Such abstract literature Ingarden terms 'pure' in its aesthetics, while drama's effects are dependent on 'an appropriate attitude' on the spectator's part (Ingarden 1973a: 321).[4] To this extent, drama should largely lie outside Ingarden's categorization of art's strata, yet he is at pains to rein them into line with literary purity at the same time as permitting various exceptions. For example, dramatic language is part of a *meaningful* representation and is therefore capable of explanation at a synoptic level. While not always fully conscious to the creator, it can be to the interpreter. I can comprehend the way that the words of Hamlet in Act 3 may relate to the strategic development of the associations that underlie his language in Act 5. Moreover, spectators are outside the world of the actors and may not share the reactions or values of the *dramatis personae* that inhabit such a context. Indeed, we have constantly the obligation of choice as to how we judge how that world functions (Ingarden 1973a: 392–3).

These approaches share an interest in aesthetic effects, but there are consequences that can diverge widely when it comes to any practical application. In short, we could build upon them in using the freedom to adapt and create using the received text as some sort of very preliminary springboard, or we could, on the other hand, place a greater emphasis on the text as setting limits and focus so that any subjectivity released in spectating or reading is given direction. Especially as regards Gadamer – in some readings – you could mix the two alternatives. 'Subjectivity' could be a suspect goal in that it can get confused with a rather solipsistic inwardness wherein what I call *Hamlet*, say, *is Hamlet* for me, and my testimony as to the impulses released by my own lights is only worth registering by others in that I set myself up as a generous and experienced spectator with a particularly acute sensitivity. Others may disagree.

For Jean-Paul Sartre, however, 'subjectivity' is a much more valuable quantity and is no given. In his late musings on the term in his lecture, 'Marxism and Subjectivity', given to Rome's Gramsci Institute in December 1961, he tried to clarify just what the search for individual freedom entailed in a world of exploitation and ideological 'certainties'; applying his argument to the subject of this study, we are formed by external forces and either surrender to the received opinions and self-definitions with which we start out when we see a play, or we find within ourselves and our personal history a more active embrace of our potential to be powerful subjects, so that art might permeate our social consciousness in a truly transformative sense. Dividing subjectivity into two alternative spheres, that of 'having-to-be' and that of 'not-knowing', Sartre opens up a necessary gap between the passive self and a receptivity that searches for some perception beyond the given. Once we confront the fact that we cannot, inevitably, grasp a totality of social being under normal circumstances, we can still step outside the conventional once we encounter an alien consciousness – or what we make of it. Put in more existentialist terms, it is a difference between the inertia encouraged by a system of existing relationships and *praxis*, the active involvement that leads to opposition and freedom: 'there is the condition of interiority, which means that the whole does not exist as an initial given, which has to be maintained, but is something that must be perpetually maintained, which must always-already be maintained' (Sartre 2016: 19).[5] As a result of this enhanced awareness or interiority, we sense what we do not know and it is literature pre-eminently that allows this perception the fullest rein. Intent on capturing this therapeutic effect, Sartre dug down into just what the impulse to write might involve in his 1948 collection of essays, *What is Literature?* Drawing a distinction between the writing of prose and of poetry, he viewed the former as favouring transitive and committed intentions, whereas the latter (and this could include drama) was more fitted for a recipient's inspection if it were considered an object. Commitment might eventually arrive from less pragmatic sources, but the crucial word here is *eventually*. Such works most certainly use language, but only to wrest its cumulative effect away from a normal set of senses – and 'good' theatre. In this process, a writer is more like an impresario, for 'the creative act is only an incomplete and abstract moment in the production of a work . . . It is the joint effort of author and reader which brings upon the scene that concrete and imaginary object which is the work of the mind' (Sartre 2001: 31). The author thereby willingly gives over to the viewer or reader the task of completion, but such an act of charity does not involve a predestined effect, for her/his obligation is to engage attention, not prescribe its destination: 'It is a question of silences which are so particular that they could not retain any meaning outside the object which the reading causes to appear' (Sartre 2001: 32). To that extent, the full effect is irreducible and goes beyond prose paraphrase, a state that permits multiple readings.

For Sartre, the theatre metaphor is indicative and, at the same time, precise where a physical theatre is in the picture. Far from escapist, the imagination is the most effective motivation for any change, both perceptual and political; otherwise, we would simply succumb to the present system and censor the capacity for envisaging change. The basic virtue of *The Imaginary* (Sartre 2004) is that it is confined not just to art, but cognition more generally. We might attend the theatre and be content with the ritual of passivity; indeed, some productions are to be consumed in that way, and they leave little trace, aside perhaps of an appreciation of craft or a confirmation of tradition. We end up, in the main, where we started. Sartre opens with a very preliminary question: what do we see when we open our eyes? Perceptually, we can break our vision down into a measurement of material objects: that is not a real palace before us, but rather plasterboard and skilfully applied paint. The imagination, however, is not tied to this form of basic observation as it exceeds the material object to summon any past experiences, for example, of courtliness, opulence and high status. We run into less obvious matters, though, when we evaluate such qualities and perhaps equate them with unethical or straitjacketed behaviour. This common (and explicable) train of associations is, largely, willed or 'motivated' by us, given what we trace as the author's use of such objects. Thus, a wood outside Athens is never a neutral figure in any production of *A Midsummer Night's Dream*. Sartre names any object that is 'imaged' an *irreality*: 'Without doubt it is present but, at the same time, it is out of reach.' In order to try to capture it, I must 'irrealise' myself; this involves a stepping out of the normative contexts that name me and render my actions predictable to others as well as myself, a resituating and so redefinition of my ego. In this, I practise a form of freedom: 'thus I can produce at will – or almost – the irreal object that I want, but I cannot make of it what I want. If I want to transform it, I must in fact create other objects; and between them there will necessarily be holes' (Sartre 2004: 125, 135). This is foundational in this sense of the 'imaginary', for we cannot segregate fully – on reflection – the object from its 'irreal' status. The actor playing Hamlet provides us with certain analogies to tragic heroism, youth, Northern European states and grief morphing into thoughtful vengefulness, but not with equal force in *this* performance, whatever the text might, in the study, give us to believe. If my mention of fictiveness is, however, deeply significant for the spectator; s/he is not deluded into confusing a plausible fiction for any pre-existent body: '[The actor] uses all his feelings, all his strength, all his gestures as analogons of the feelings and conduct of Hamlet. But by this fact he irrealizes them. *He lives entirely in a irreal world*' (Sartre 2004: 191). Far from this being some sort of evasiveness, the play that we perceive (or the music or painting we contemplate) invites a response of this kind, an invitation to recreate or complete – and this is a deep instance of how the imagination in general cannot be compartmentalized. It inevitably functions in the most direct of perceptions and – to a lesser or greater degree – transforms our world.[6]

So far there has only been an implicit mention of psychoanalytic theories of response. In that such considerations merit studies on their own, their place within this preliminary survey of response I have limited mainly to attempts to measure cognitive responses to effects and how they promote emotions that underlie later rationalizations in externalized criticism and evaluation. As Carolyn E. Brown has it, literature can 'resemble psychoanalysis by helping repressed feelings to surface into consciousness', and, as a consequence, we are more capable of detecting preconscious and unconscious factors that confirm likes and dislikes, aside from more obvious and generalized appreciations of the craft of narrative construction and poetic distinctiveness (Brown 2015: 16).[7] The less prepared-for responses can be the most effective in that they penetrate our senses before we can deflect them by claiming that they are irrelevant (to the conscious mind) or just simply too eccentric. In Chapter 3, we will encounter in a more sociological sense how we enter a theatre or other fora as part of an 'interpretive community' or armed with certain 'competences'. The role of response analysis in these instances is to bring to light preconscious allegiances that determine any aesthetic qualities in response.

What can get lost in these approaches are the more visceral experiences of recoil or embrace that occur quite outside any effort of will or decision. Any theatrical training involves an exposure to embodied performance where a gesture or choreography or melody (or all three) communicate in and around any given script. We are aiming here at an attempt to articulate, as Amy Cook puts it, a 'paradigm shift that keeps trying to arrive', which is about 're-categorising what we are talking about when we talk about thinking, or meaning, or touching, or feeling, or embodiment, or performance' (Cook 2013: 84).[8] Thus, any stage is not populated by things as such, no matter how lifelike they may appear, but rather affective material; characters may appear comprehensible as types, but it would be bland theatre if we were encouraged to pigeonhole them as consistent throughout a performance. At base, it is also worth exploring the world of difference between recordings of Shakespeare (even those streamed through to us from live performance elsewhere) and a bodily encounter before us.

In Bruce McConachie's work, recent emphases in cognitive science are placed in the service of audience analysis. A useful starting point is his essay, 'Cognitive Studies and Epistemic Competence in Cultural History: Moving Theatre Studies beyond Freud and Lacan' (McConachie 2006), where he stresses the role played – adapted from Mary Fulbrook's *Historical Theory: Ways of Imagining the Past* (Fulbrook 2002) – of a historian's choice (or at least membership) of a 'paradigm community' (McConachie 2006: 51–75). By enlisting an initial shared paradigm with an expected audience (McConachie's example is the case of why the blacked-up 'wenches' – male impersonators of comic female characters – were so fashionable in mid-nineteenth-century minstrel entertainments), he isolates the need for such displays to dip into an audience's 'epistemic competence' – their openness to imagine what they may not have directly experienced. By simulating how they were entertainment material, by embodying their activity and tricks of the stage, one can move beyond historiography and psychoanalysis.[9] McConachie, however, does not typify audience behaviour throughout any one performance; the most provoking experiences are those that keep a spectator on edge and for this to occur most effectively, we must be prepared to accept reversals or unforeseen extensions of our first-act knowledge (for example) in order to maintain this alertness. We thereby might question and look back upon first impressions. For this to happen, though, we need to have some recognition of what McConachie terms the 'affordances' of any action – the sometimes unacknowledged bases for recognition that theatre has the potential to unearth by subverting them or taking them into unexpected directions.[10] Shakespeare's fools such as Feste and Lear's companion resist any attempts to have us understand their world completely, and this resistance to a deciphering permeates and spills over other apparently disconnected episodes within the play.

The words in a script may also create their own range of 'affordances', but the thrust of the approach is not to unthinkingly fall back on inherited familiarities or to expect (and favour) them so as to resist new connotations. In McConachie's *Evolution, Cognition, and Performance* (2015), this elasticity of response is provided out of an appreciation of 'play' (akin to Gadamer's sense) from what appears to be child's eyes: the movement in and out of character, the sinuousness of narrative impetus, for example. This aptness for a 'blending' of concepts, the trying on of a variety of roles and ideas, dissociates us from a customary grasp of life and its social conditioning (McConachie 2015: 35–53).[11] All too easily, the corporeal gets excised from a consideration of any theatrical experience: for example, the setting of contracts between spectator and actor that include the announcement of running time, the suitability of seats (if there are any), the placing of the interval or the proximity of the action where there is the threat or opportunity of direct involvement. A film or recording cannot provide this; indeed, they are not designed to. What emerges as of particular impact in cognitive terms are assessments of how that proximity is handled, how the mood changes strike us, how opportunities for direct vocal address and involvement are provided, and how the action is segmented (that is, how our attention is elongated or truncated by long or short scenes). There is consequently a tendency to concentrate on these physiological effects that emerge from individual performances or productions, even night by night. We can testify to our own feelings and hope that these are not too eccentric or accidental so as to infer that this might be true of others who attended on another night or whose perspective might have differed significantly given the possibility that their sight lines were not blocked, their seats in a gallery or balcony foreshortened the view, or one encountered the performance in the right mood. What one can attempt to theorize is opportunity rather than content. As Norman N. Holland terms it, there is a 'content fallacy' in one's preconceptions, where one is prepared only to search for what is 'in' the text rather than for what we can authentically feel because of it (Holland 2009: 171–86). Where any drama is concerned, one has to imagine that one has contact with the 'text' in the most authentic sense in the moment, deliberately attempting to deny its published existence.

The problems that more abstract readings of Shakespeare plays encounter are twofold: they tend to institute ideal performances as templates that are eventually limiting in that they are not designed so as to take into account the physical incursions of performances as physical events, and, just as significantly, they ignore the circumstances in which meaning takes place, which is transactive rather than informative. The materiality of performance can be regarded as merely the packaging of the spoken content, yet in Erika T. Lin's terms, it involves an awareness of the boundaries of theatrical performance, whereby we note the permeability of what constitutes drama and also the values then as now of entertainment, including the part played by song and jig (Lin 2012: 41–69, 107–33). I will return to some of these issues in Chapter 4 when I focus on *The Tempest* and the potential to resist spectacle and ritualized spectating. As Mary Thomas Crane observes, cognitive responses to Shakespearean action and its effects are notoriously complex to map because they predate and so are apt to pre-empt conscious evaluation and the attendant processing that is the basis of consciousness. Once there is the attempt to bring into the light certain nontextual features and possibilities derived from a text, one gets nearer to the theatrical conditions for meaning and, one hopes, the assumptions with which Shakespeare operated and his theatrical commentators now take as a necessary challenge (Crane 2001: 3–35). Susan Bennett's agenda is an attractive one: an attempt to locate how we might foster an independence of reaction that leads to the deepest grounds for pleasure even while enjoying a collective appreciation. Matters of 'good' and 'bad', in aesthetic terms, often run up against 'aesthetic codes as culturally determined' (Bennett 1997: 155) and this tests our determination to interrogate the desirability of such codes.

2

The Role of the Spectator and Reader

There are episodes in *Antony and Cleopatra* that encourage the purist to regard them as theatrically clumsy, or at least a staging challenge. One of the most notorious scenes occurs when the dying Antony joins Cleopatra atop the monument in 4.15. The effort required to haul his body up to his queen and her attendants would surely distract from the mournful and elegiac mood the text demands: 'Here's sport indeed! How heavy weighs my lord! / Our strength is all gone into heaviness; / That makes the weight' (4.15.33–5). What could have been a choice of 'heavy' as sad is here defeated or at least translated into a pun where the sheer physical weight is linked to tragic fate. Moreover, the onlookers' chorus 'Ah, heavy sight!' (4.15.42) emphasizes the literal spectacle of moving him up to the gallery, taken to be the roof of Cleopatra's monument. She plus Charmian and Alexas had entered the scene '*aloft*' (*s.d.*, 4.15.0). The Guard that brought Antony onstage at 4.15.10 cannot be taken to be alongside the women (as there would be no room for that), so that involves a deliberately complex piece of stagecraft in order that the lovers, in their final moments together, might hold each other. Presumably at 4.15.38, there has to be a means whereby the body (for Antony must be now a nearly dead weight) makes it up the ten feet or so and probably the extra three over the gallery balustrade.

This is to say nothing of the practical problem as to how to remove his body at the scene's end.

This detail is taken from Plutarch's *Lives of the Noble Grecians and Romans* as translated by Sir Thomas North (1579), the principal source for the play: his body was carried 'in his mens armes into the entry of the monument'. Given Cleopatra's reluctance to open the gates, she at first makes contact through the 'high windowes'. Throwing down 'certaine chaines and ropes', she anticipates a 'trussed' Antony delivered to her by the efforts of herself and 'two women only'. Onlookers agreed that they had never beheld 'so pitiful a sight', noting his bloody appearance, and they also felt empathy with the women, for it was a 'hard thing', and especially for the queen, for she used all 'her strength to her uttermost power' to bring Antony to her (see Bullough 1957–75: 5:309–10.) What might convince a reader as to a 'pitiful sight' does not translate to the feelings a spectator might experience. Here we have the effort and motive (but note the sign of self-preservation in not opening the gates) but no reliable hint as to how it could be dramatic. There is a voluminous theatre history of the play that has addressed the issue of practicalities (Lamb 1980: 180–5);[1] for our purposes, it might be as well to dwell on its intentional awkwardness, principally a reflection upon the 'sport' that Cleopatra indicates, whereby their 'strength is all gone into heaviness' (4.15.34) – detail that is calculated to produce a dissonance of some kind.

Shakespeare was under no obligation to adopt the Plutarch account literally, but there is an attempt so to do. What we are left with might just be explained more expertly in the future by perhaps intensive work on Blackfriars or Globe theatre construction, but the more recent spectators (and I would argue, early modern audiences) were still placed in a position whereby a possible apogee of pity might be offset by physical contrivance: the world does not immediately stop in its tracks to behold the sorry sight. This is neither an isolated nor a local perspective. The tableau of Cleopatra's corpse is described for us by Charmian and she is called a 'lass unparalleled'. Her crown must also have been dislodged in her death throes, for it is clear that Charmian notes that it is 'awry' (5.2.315, 317).[2] The dialectal diminutive of 'lass' (Northern/Midland term for girl; *OED*) clashes with the alternative drive to display a regal icon of tragic destiny.

Without involving response theories, text-centred criticism has frequently perceived the split in the play between satiric framing and heroic display and between *realpolitik* and a heterocosm of desire and dream. This proceeds as much from Enobarbus's dual role as acerbic observer and, especially where Cleopatra is concerned, disarmed admirer, as the clash of perspectives embedded in individual scenes. Philo's Roman commentary on Antony's ensnarement in 'a gipsy's lust' (1.1.10) hits us first before Antony and Cleopatra's towering verse about transcendent love, where 'kingdoms are clay' (1.1.36). The alternation between a world of Roman duty and Egyptian release is even signalled in the list of the 'Persons of the Play' in later Folio versions. As a way of describing – and so of a coming to terms with – the play, Rome might indeed be the Rome of the history books and Plutarch's records. It has a geographical location and could be said to exist outside of a subjective appropriation. There are connotations that seem fixed – or why else might Shakespeare have chosen references that have preformed associations? This reduction of the fiction to a segment of a history lesson is attractive to those who would prefer to pin meanings down so as to establish accuracy of perspective and to do away with the nebulousness of projection on the part of the interpreter.

Where this play is concerned, the variety of possibilities challenge any single line of access to the play. It may seem to be the conventional elegy that Octavius provides at the play's close, where the 'great solemnity' (5.2.364) of their funeral seems an act of closure that grants Antony and Cleopatra due reverence as tragic types. One might pause once we realize that it is Octavius – the victor – uttering these lines and that there is also a victory for 'solemn show' (5.2.362), the Roman virtues that, if we peered into our chronicles, we would also find spelling the death of the Republic. To the victor the spoils and what we more clearly view is a stage cleared of bodies, where the 'high events' of their death actually lend a glory to 'those who make them' and where their tragedy might in effect reflect well on those who caused it: 'No less in pity than his glory which / Brought them to be lamented' (5.2.360–1). The temptation to smooth out these complexities can bring in its wake a lack of perceptiveness about the ironies of the drama and its precise verbal and gestural form. For studies of audience reception, the most instructive focus is on how we process the deeper recesses of the portrayed action. Leaving aside experiences that confuse us because, on close inspection, they are ill expressed or misty in conception, the most memorable experiences might be those that we feel and sense are novel and/or provocative.

Hans Robert Jauss introduces a significant set of considerations not only as regards theatre and literary history, but also how meaning is produced theatrically. His sense of a 'horizon of expectations' that any audience cannot help but bring with them to the playtext does not solely derive from a narrow dramatic corridor but rather from the layout of the whole house, sociologically, religiously and politically. The experience may occur in the playhouse but analysis of its impact is not confined to inspecting specific cultures of spectating and acting; moreover, the icon of 'Shakespeare' draws in so many preconceptions of cultural value that the expectations are deeply set and immensely influential. As Jauss notes, history and aesthetics are entwined: we might find a representation significant and moving, but it is worth spending time attending to one's context and angle of approach, conceding that there is a point of entry to meaning that is already conditioned; what arrests the attention is not an effect of free individual choice. Post-Holocaust, it may just be possible to identify Shylock in *The Merchant of Venice* as risible and his fate deserved, but it is surely not easy so to do or feel. Katherine's taming in *The Taming of the Shrew* now needs apology or dramatic conjuring so that contemporary audiences might find it acceptable in its most literal forms.

The example of *Antony and Cleopatra* might illustrate the value of Jauss's comments. Safely within the confines of a viewing experience where cultural capital is assured – at the Royal Shakespeare Theatre or even nowadays at Shakespeare's Globe – the play is known as one of the most valued of Shakespeare's tragedies and thus potentially as one of his most esteemed achievements. Added to that, there is a certain cultural construction of expectation that brings in notions of empire, classicism, race and gender – not programmatically, as if we were more insistent at this moment than they were in the past and that they now strike us more forcibly. The play, however, has not always been accepted unproblematically or even viewed regularly. Its complex structure has been an obstacle, veering between Alexandria and Rome, where choric scenes jostle more heroic attitudes and satire works to displace epic display. Any evidence of its Jacobean staging is thin and in the later years of the seventeenth century it was supplanted by more 'correct' and unified versions of the story: Sir Charles Sedley's *Antony and Cleopatra* (Duke's Theatre, Dorset Garden, 1677) and John Dryden's *All For Love; or, the World Well Lost* (Theatre Royal, Drury Lane, 1678). Even when it was rediscovered by David Garrick in 1759 (at Drury Lane), it was as a vehicle for pageantry and costly set-pieces; as a result, the forty-plus scenes (according to Nicholas Rowe's editorial work) were reduced to just twenty-seven, and the text was only partially Shakespeare's as the action was adopted from the combined efforts of Garrick and Edward Capell in the production of a truncated edition (1758). A distrust of the Folio text persisted in Kemble's and Macready's attempts to reintroduce an 'original' version in 1813 (Covent Garden) and 1833 (Drury Lane) respectively. Kemble lost the galley scene – a necessity if one were to dispense with the character of Pompey – and both the Soothsayer and Clown; he also interpolated portions of Dryden's text unannounced. Macready compressed the action to just seventeen scenes and Dryden peeps throughout the fourth and fifth acts. He thought nothing of moving Enobarbus's now most famous description of the lovers' first meeting (2.2.201–50) as a frontispiece to their first entry.

For Jauss, this recourse to a historicist set of enquiries is not merely to provide an unmotivated narrative; using reading as his default, he often relies on radical approaches that place a lower emphasis on gesture and visualization. At root, he is concerned to excavate radical features lying often dormant within a text, the realization of which tells us as much about the historical location of a meaning-event as about the text's implications itself. Value accrues to isolating 'a new form in the literary series' (one could substitute 'theatrical') pitted against a general intuition that there were 'worn-out forms, artistic devices, and genres' that could suddenly seem to a modern eye and ear inauthentic. These 'pass into the background until at a new moment in the evolution they are made "perceptible" once again' (Jauss 1982a: 33). These early theatrical 'readings' have to try to adapt to survive. Spectacle (the battle at Actium, Cleopatra's entry, the exoticism of Egypt, for example) pads out, and distracts from, a text that was regarded as fractured and generically too hybrid. Richard Madelaine's compendious account of the production decisions facing directors is as much about the limits placed on choice by pragmatic factors such as size of auditorium, the finances available to provide set-piece grandeur, and the taste for exact scenic detail as about alternations in critical fashion.

Yet what is the primary driver for such changes in aesthetic demand? Theatrical opportunism or compromise stalk any drive for radical intervention, yet the staging of plays is also part of a dialectic, an answer to a perceived desire to re-evaluate that ultimately stems from outside the literary/artistic sphere, but that in turn is fostered by dramatic restlessness. Any divide between 'aesthetic' and 'historical knowledge' can be bridged once we realize that plays do not simply offer themselves to a general historical placement (and are pigeonholed according to what they are likely to have meant to, say, a typical Victorian or millennial viewer), but, alternatively, that they have the capacity to be 'socially formative' and that they contribute to any account of evolving social change. Thereby, art 'competes with other arts and social forces in the emancipation of mankind from its natural, religious, and social bonds' (Jauss 1982a: 69). Instead, therefore, of relying on an agenda that requires mere artistic competence and a consumerist adequacy, we search for what might be the awkwardness of emancipation and an alertness to new experience. Hermeneutically speaking, this can only be realized by an act of intervention, whereby radical novelty is a surprise, an unforeseen response to a 'problem left behind to which the new work in the historical series is the answer' (Jauss 1982a: 34). Any historical moment is not just simply contemporary and apprehended in the present, but is regarded through the lens of past exempla. Thus, any 'past horizon of old and new forms, problems and solutions, is only recognizable in its further mediation within the present horizon of the received work' (Jauss 1982a: 34), and it is only realized reliably out of the interpreter's 'experience'.

In returning to *Antony and Cleopatra*, what has been inherited as too complex, in both structural and ethical terms, could be answers to questions that had not been present to us. What Sedley and Dryden had 'solved' should have remained tantalizing and even irritating. When we turn to Dryden's 'Preface' to *All For Love*, we find him determined to rescue the action of Shakespeare's narrative by pointing to 'the excellency of the moral', whereby 'unlawful love' brought about an 'unfortunate' end; Samuel Johnson was startled by the way that one's 'curiosity was always busy' and the 'passions always interested', not a clear virtue because he found also that the 'events' were 'produced without any art of connection or care of disposition' (Vickers 1974–95: 1:163, 5:148). While both William Hazlitt and Samuel Taylor Coleridge admired the passion depicted in the later scenes, they were also conscious that it overflowed the measure, enacting the irresponsibility that was depicted (Hazlitt 2009: 78, 83; Coleridge 1960: 1:77). By 1857, and Charles Bathurst's *Remarks on the Differences in Shakespeare's Versification*, this lack of moderation stemmed from a carelessness in the writing, 'with no attempt at dignity' (Bathurst 1837: 130). Anticipating Jauss's attempt at an analysis of such stage history, then, we could glean at least two concerns that come into view – and then recede – begging particular attention: the play's thwarted attempt at epic scope, and its lack of structural consistency. For Jauss, the aesthetics of reception (*Rezeptionsästhetik*) is a method of locating symptoms of cultural change that most other modes of enquiry miss, so the questions that emerge from observing how the most troublesome aspects of the new work – or radical interpretation – are not to be confused with an account of steady evolution. The crucial literary historical narrative brings into relief contradiction and at times revisioning. Indeed, if one limits one's focus to the reception of just one play (however rich its cultural traces) or, in a wider conspectus, how certain literary forms survive and respond throughout general history (the most central concern in Jauss's later writing), then one discovers how relative to a wider history aesthetic judgements are; one cannot respond in any transcendent sense to art laying claim to universal values or senses, for one should be responsive to how the relationship between text and spectator – materially and ideologically – varies in the production of meaning.

For example, the apogee of the more decorative and grandiose reading of the play's potential was evident in the early twentieth century, wherein Herbert Beerbohm Tree (His Majesty's, 1906) and Frank Benson in his 1912 revival of the Stratford 1898 version treated the audience to an experience lasting some four-and-a-half hours. Spectacle came at a cost, therefore, as changes of scene (and there were many) often entailed the dropping of the curtain and some backstage commotion. It was not long before the memory that Shakespeare might not have solely provided us with an Olympian panorama, full of majestic characters, took hold. The focus on how Plutarch (in Sir Thomas North's translation) described the tragic characters in the sunset of their years rather than in their pomp led to a less sublime spectacle, bordering on a more intimate view of declining powers and judgement. It was also known – but ignored – that the Lord Chamberlain's records for 1669 had claimed that it was 'formerly acted at the Blackfriars', a less imposing private arena that Shakespeare's company often used during the winter months from 1606 onwards. What seems obvious is only so because it is designed to 'fit'. One might also ask the question: does this travel historically as the same play throughout?

At the core of Jauss's challenge to theory is the emphasis on how aesthetics cannot stand apart from historical conditioning; we might feel as well as judge that there is quality in an artefact, yet that is not derived from any universal ingredient in the work that should move a spectator. Far from it, we receive meanings and give them emotional colouring because we are where we are in the flow of history. Thus it follows that we have to grant that any work does not directly reflect its moment of inception, but rather acts upon it. As a consequence, a literary or a dramatic history should be based rather on 'the relationship of work to work' alongside any relation 'between work and mankind'. Ultimately, 'the historical coherence of works among themselves must be seen in the interrelations of production and reception' (Jauss 1982a: 15). However far we progress in our understanding of initial theatrical conditions, what was evident to one audience is only part of the recognition of our own horizons of comprehension. Critical understanding must proceed aside from any search for an objective account or consistent basis for verification. In this, there is a dialogical relationship that any text forms with its audiences or readers, whereby a 'philological understanding can exist only in a perpetual confrontation with the text, and cannot be allowed to be reduced to a knowledge of facts' (Jauss 1982a: 21). What the dictionary helps us get to grips with is preliminary: where this text takes the words and where this performance acts upon them is what most engages Jauss. Our perceptions of this are, however, historically conditioned as much by the 'works already read' as the cultural expectations we now confront and – perhaps unthinkingly – accept: 'the obvious historical implication of this is that the understanding of the first reader will be sustained and enriched in a chain of receptions from generation to generation' (Jauss 1982a: 20). We cannot escape a web of allusion or pun or echo that renders art an aesthetic experience. The past is with us even if it cannot be ultimately determining.

The artistic content of any form of words or implied gestures involves our, first, allowing ourselves to be aware of these contextual pressures, and then resisting them to reach for an altered 'horizon'. Not all 'art' is significant in this regard, for it may be that we cling to the familiar (and are encouraged by the text so to do) so that a 'ruling standard of taste' remains intact (even confirmed). As such, the experience is hardly exceptional and would not therefore figure in any history. Change is effected by not just the choice of radical form or rhetoric but by a modification of the audience's semantic 'horizon', and that cannot be exemplified by even the closest of textual inspection, as the register for real literary historical change emerges from reaction, not genesis. Moreover, unless we strive to comprehend this predisposition of approach on the part of the reader/spectator, we will fail to find the path to registering a text's impact, to realize just what answers are being supplied by the text to questions (cultural, political, psychological) to which a first audience were attracted. No writer creates so as not to be heard, so, implicated in this search, we delve into that 'audience-in-the-head' that motivates (unconsciously sometimes) any writer: 'the reconstruction of the horizon of expectations, in the face of which a work was created and received in the past, enables one on the other hand to pose questions that the text gave an answer to, and thereby to discover how the contemporary reader could have viewed and understood the work' (Jauss 1982a: 28). This dynamic affects also our own horizon in that the past is what we know or more readily recognize.

When accounting for reception of any kind, there should be a gathering realization that we are set in a situation in the present and that is always there due to the reading of a received past. Consequently, if there is an authentic aesthetic perception that we – at our most alert – attain when we read self-consciously, then there is the potential for a modification of the 'horizon' we have inherited, both personally and communally. There is 'general' history – the usual material we consult to help us locate any writing in an original terrain – and then there is the 'special' history that affects behaviour and that issues from us. Jauss does offer the hope that any 'literary experience' might permeate a 'lived praxis' in its capacity for preforming our 'understanding of the world' with the ability to speak to customary 'social behaviour' (Jauss 1982a: 39). An active reader or spectator enables her/himself to envisage change not only in breaking away from the critical and cultural past but also in recognizing or altering customary assumptions.

This is an attractive proposition and Jauss lays great store by this positive aesthetic attitude that is produced by reflections that are daring and in which we invest personality and imagination. 'Aesthetic interest' – in Jauss's sense – moves beyond a 'mere gawking at the new' but rather it is 'more a new kind of seeing which functions as discovery' (Jauss 1982b: 4). We hit here a potential problem in that any transition to a new 'horizon' can only be accurately assessed once the actual definition of 'horizon' is redefined – not as simply 'context' but in the light of an emergence of new aesthetic experience. Noting a 'horizon' is to grasp limits and blind spots that centre a grouping of pre-given assumptions so that 'sense' might be made of a text and its value. In the opening chapter of *Aesthetic Experience and Literary Hermeneutics* (Jauss 1982b), Jauss outlines a specimen history of this kind in his 'Sketch of a Theory and History of Aesthetic Experience'. Matters under investigation include any transformations of what populate terms such as 'art', 'author', 'text' and even the 'aesthetic' that preside over how evaluation might take place and how works address any readership and audience. These basic considerations are the principal focus and not any transhistorical application of values. To that extent, the registering of a degree of pleasure or consonance is no sure guide to the more significant events that should mark out literary historical change. As compass bearings in this history, Jauss signals three regular aspects of a literary history: *poiesis* (the constitution of how the 'producing consciousness' creates its own world), *aesthesis* (more to do with the 'receiving consciousness' and how perceptions may be altered by the aesthetic process) and *catharsis* (how the transformative power of emotional involvement might be produced and to what end). For our purposes the bias will be towards the definition and effect of considering aesthesis, always admitting that Jauss does not ultimately regard the avenue of enquiry as separate. Indeed, catharsis is integral with what we might do as a result of deep feelings and identifications that emerge from the reception of literature. Once we trace the impulse to 'break the hold of the real world', two types of reaction might result: either a 'free, moral identification with an exemplary action', or a regression into 'a state of pure curiosity' (and nothing more – Jauss 1982b: 96).

Specific to theatre, however, Jauss notes how the collective power of instant reaction might have a power that other forms of reception may not. From a wider perspective, say, in the topos of *theatrum mundi*, the metaphors of 'play' and 'theatre' mean something linked but not identical to any dramatic happening. We enjoy for a sacred interval, in the playhouse, a double sense of self – the playful assumptions of new roles alongside a consciousness that we will surrender them to reality once the spell is broken. 'the aesthetic relationship to a role ... does not differ in kind from habitual or engaged behaviour in a social role. It merely makes contrastively conscious the doubling that is inherent in all role behaviour and makes it possible to enjoy oneself in the experience of a role' (Jauss 1982b: 138). By stepping outside of our inherited social status and the assumptions that lock it into place, even if temporarily, we thereby get a glimpse of a progressive future and make of the work in question a live document.

Central to a history of how *Antony and Cleopatra* was regarded is a consideration of just what portions were seen and what staging choices occluded or highlighted. Certainly, the overblown and perhaps deliberately distracting pomp accorded those of high status or exotic heritage obscured even those attempts at providing a fuller (Folio) text. It also obstructed the less reassuring perspective on the portrayal of cultural decay. Drawing on a pervasive mood of decline, it was in the immediate post-war theatre that the play could not help but refer outwards to – for Britain – the Suez crisis of 1956. Some of the most nationalist impulses released by the isolation and shame of the events led to adverse comments on any attempt to render Cleopatra 'un-English' in her Oriental eroticism; for example, Robert Helpmann's 1957 production at the Old Vic tried to escape the trap of star casting to include two relatively unknown (and thereby naïve) protagonists – Keith Michell and Margaret Whiting (aged 30 and 24 respectively) – so that the 'infinite variety' ascribed to Cleopatra by Enobarbus (2.2.246) came over as juvenile fickleness, and an unformed search for one's own character. A Western gaze on the East surfaces also, especially when there have been increases in archaeological evidence such as the immense popularity of the British Museum's Tutankhamun exhibition of 1972 in London that ran along a revival of glittering costumes in Trevor Nunn's attempt at the Memorial Theatre in Stratford-upon-Avon. The cultural distance of an Egyptian feminist, however, could help a boldness in Janet Suzman's portrayal that at times puzzled and unsettled Richard Johnson's Antony.

As Jauss brings to our notice, there is never a steady state perspective that helps us appreciate what is 'in' the play. The present is not the summation of other epochs; it is inevitably different and inflects the play's language in contemporary senses. Updating a Shakespeare play has only relatively recently been acceptable, perhaps since Tony Richardson's Bankside Globe version of 1973, but, lacking the majesty of an imperial past, the cocktail dresses out of *Vogue* and smart tuxedos struck several as near parody rather than reverential commemoration (see Madelaine 1998: 109–11). Indeed, this is the risk taken by smaller-scale versions, such as Peter Brook's in 1978 (RSC, Stratford) and Adrian Noble's in 1982 (The

Other Place, Stratford), both attuned more to personal relationships than their imperial consequences. For Brook, his manipulative Cleopatra brought out Glenda Jackson's imperious changes of mood that both attracted Alan Howard as Antony and kept him in thrall. Even Jonathan Pryce (as Octavius) and Patrick Stewart (Enobarbus) were rarely granted a position at centre stage once Jackson was present. Its running length of three hours and fifty minutes was largely due to Brook's determination to allow a number of otherwise minor parts their time in the sun, bringing to the fore Octavius's vulnerability and Enobarbus's shocked fascination at Eastern excess. Even his Lepidus and Pompey rose above being ciphers to the grand imperial theme in their measured (and tragically ironic) assessments of their hopes and dreams. The pared-down Other Place had spectators in close contact – in the round – with the action; a stark black-and-white design was almost claustrophobic, especially in the Egyptian scenes all played on the lower level, spilling out into the audience at times, while the Roman world of principle and political deliberation existed further away in the upper gallery.

It is also a step change to register how daring it used to be to cast an actor of colour to play Cleopatra (as also Othello or Aaron from *Titus Andronicus*). The more fringe attempts to render the play as of urgent contemporary value are where we find this ambition. Estelle Parsons's 1979 adaptation (Interart Theatre, New York) was bilingual: Hispanic actors were Romans whereas English was spoken by the predominantly white-skinned Egyptians. The attempt to play with concepts of 'alien' identities came to the fore in Michael Kahn's attempt to illustrate division and racial mistrust (1988, Shakespeare Theatre, Washington, DC) by casting a black Franchelle Dorn as Cleopatra against a white (and British) Kenneth Haigh as Antony. The clash of acting styles included the – to some – distracting alternatives on display in verse speaking. Dorn's attempt at naturalistic delivery provided an antidote to Haigh's orotund accents. In Britain, the colour bar was lifted for Cleopatra in 1989 but, admittedly, in a heavily adapted version,

Cleopatra and Antony, directed by Malcolm Edwards for the Actors Touring Company that was set in the 1930s. Pauline Black came from an unorthodox heritage: a singer with the Ska band, The Selector, working on the contrast (to the Romans' disadvantage) with Patrick Wilde's nervy Antony (doubled with the Clown) and Susan Henry's visibly repressed Octavia. Reduced to a cast of only five, there were passages lifted from Plutarch and Dryden. To date, it is far more likely to have coloured actors tackling Cleopatra or, indeed, an all-black cast – even if that tends to remove any evident clash of race (see Yvonne Brewster's 1991 production for the Merseyside Everyman Theatre and Taiwa Theatre Company).[3] Companies still tend to be tentative about raising race issues: a coloured Cleopatra summons a Shakespearean inventory of typecast characteristics, incorporating, to Western sensibilities, fickleness and inscrutable sensual behaviour. A 'white' Antony is caught between such new possibilities and his inherited obligation to be Roman as regards duty and the rites of power. If one is not careful, racist stereotypes are confirmed as heroic, even if tragic. When Tarell Alvin McCraney 'edited' his production of the play in a touring version (Swan Theatre, Stratford-upon-Avon, 2013), he set it in a Napoleonic colonialist context in Haiti, where the oppressed native population were the black Egyptians and the French the Romans. Joaquina Kalukango was a diminutive Cleopatra against a tall and muscular Jonathan Cake and several critics regretted the absence of Cleopatra's imperial status.[4] A similar ambition to run against expectations could be found in the casting of the immensely experienced Kathryn Hunter as Michael Boyd's Cleopatra (RSC, The Courtyard Theatre, 2010). Short (and white), Hunter was tantalizing in her mercurial changes of mood and witty clipped delivery. Darrell D'Silva as her Antony was captivated less by classical beauty (he neglects the more typically attractive Sophie Russell as Octavia) than by an inscrutable set of traits; chasing her around the bare stage, it was as if he wanted to cage her. When the RSC next attempted the play, the stately and majestic

Josette Simon (dir. Iqbal Khan, Memorial Theatre, Stratford-upon-Avon, 2017) even came near to captivating Ben Allen as Octavius. Anthony Byrne as Antony was distracted even when in Rome.

This is not an attempt at a stage history in that it is not a comprehensive chronology. On the contrary, following Jauss's prescription for locating 'horizons of expectations', it falls short of claiming excellence of any one version, for each is intended meaningful for particular auditors and we should be wary of dismissing an adaptation or even the most faithful rendition by a transhistorical standard of value. Indeed, we could regard even those production choices that seem awkward or unmotivated as attempts to break free of cultural constraints, whereby we might, in instinctively rejecting them or registering discomfort, discover more about the play we have been conditioned to expect and ourselves in the process. The most valuable experience derives from this 'doubling' of selves produced by a determination to experience the new and thus contrast it with the customary 'real' that is waiting for us outside the theatre. Rome and Egypt are ultimately signifiers and it is salutary to realize how many occasions we do not encounter the full or unamended Folio text in the theatre. The impulse to make the play over to ourselves allows us to register just what is involved in that move – and just why some ur-Shakespeare is insufficent.

The shortcuts towards intelligibility are often culturally produced so as to be immediately acceptable and more easily consumable. For Wolfgang Iser, most of the connections that fill gaps in any worthwhile narrative call for a reader's involvement, and the works that repay the closest study are those that co-opt the reader/spectator in a variety of ways and via methods that make a virtue of imagining what a 'complete' and multifaceted reading might be. The balancing act of hitting just the right note of enticing suggestiveness does not involve a tantalizing display for its own sake, for it should serve a greater good: an enhanced perception that is produced out of the most complex fictions that there is a more profound imaginative reality. Iser's most famous studies of the role of implication in a reader's or spectator's experience are *The Implied Reader: Patterns of Communication in Prose Fiction from Bunyan to Beckett* (1974) and *The Act of Reading: A Theory of Aesthetic Response* (1978), although he was to open up his response theories to embrace drama later in his career. A work that explains too much might stunt a response; indeed, all fictive texts cannot supply an exhaustive array of details about their referents as they are fictional (and such superfluity would lead to stultifying redundancy). Any radical attempt to do this, such as in Sterne's *Tristram Shandy* or portions of Joyce's *Ulysses*, are formal experiments that eventually illustrate the impossibility that literature can reproduce the encyclopedic details of non-literary perception. There have to be shortcuts that involve the reader in piecing together some aspects that are not directly expressed. In terms of *Antony and Cleopatra*, individual scenes are not designed to be tightly connected to even neighbouring episodes in that any succession of actions must imply at the same time as unfurl a narrative shape.

Although initially focused on how readers respond, Iser's ideas are of value where drama is in question, especially more generally where a phenomenological approach might guide our attention. Literary communication is not functional in the way that the normal mode operates. Its conventions are far less definable and convergent: 'Literary texts . . . require a resolution of indeterminacies but, by definition, for fiction there can be no such given frames of reference. On the contrary, the reader must first discover for himself [*sic*] the code underlying the text, and this is tantamount to bringing out the meaning' (Iser 1978a: 60). One might modify this assertion by noting that if the reader is handed such a role, then the sense produced might be 'a' meaning, no matter how discoverable the schemata of the work might be. We therefore require an investigation into the process of interaction between text and reader; we process the text at a basic level, perhaps on first reading, merely to get a skeletal outline of plot, yet this does not come near to realizing – or concretizing – the depths of the *aesthetic* possibilities inherent in the reading process. For Iser, there are two poles of understanding in such an analysis: the artistic and the aesthetic. There is the art we can register when reading that is derived from the author's skill and how the work is ordered, and then there is the realization of this detail that is accomplished by the reader:

> In view of this polarity, it is clear that the work itself cannot be identical with the text or with the concretization, but must be situated somewhere between the two. It must inevitably be virtual in character, as it cannot be reduced to the reality of the text or to the subjectivity of the reader, and it is from this virtuality that it derives its dynamism.
>
> ISER 1978A: 21

These invitations to breathe life into the text should be accepted. Any work established as a preferred version by textual editors and/or located as emerging from a particular cultural context by literary historians does not provide a static range of senses: 'As the reader passes through the various perspectives offered by the text and relates the different views and patterns to one another he sets the work in motion, and so sets himself in motion too' (Iser 1978a: 21). The 'gaps' or 'blanks' are inexorably experienced by the reader within a process of 'making sense'. Any recourse to a supposition as to what a text is *supposed* to communicate is therefore a starting point, not a destination.

Iser's term for these creative individuals is that they are Implied Readers, yet the spectrum of such responses is not freely and autonomously chosen, for they are conditioned by a set of 'predispositions' that are 'laid down, not by an empirical outside reality, but by the text itself'. Consequently, such a reader is a 'construct and in no way to be identified with any real reader' (Iser 1978a: 34). A 'real' reading experience might be a passive one, where we might simply consume the narrative, not strive to step outside its apparent intentions.

Heritage Shakespeare certainly exists and it aims to soothe by pre-emptively confirming the traditional shaping that unadventurous performances obey: for example, *Antony and Cleopatra* is a tragedy, and, referring back to Aristotle's template, its exclusive focus should be on the plight of great, but flawed, individuals. Hence the action does not provoke reflection on any issue beyond that and its portrayal of tragic agony projects a pity and empathy divorced from any focus on political structures or the machinations of power and authority. If this were the case, then the un-Roman bathos of how both lovers are portrayed surely takes off some of that emotional power and dilutes the tragedy.

Iser, however, with prose narrative principally in mind, goes further than this in investigating how fluid the text's series of implications might be; far from arriving at a steady *gestalt* of the text's meaning, where we are always destined to arrive at an architectural unity where all falls into place, the most valuable narratives place us more like 'a traveller in a stagecoach who has to make out the often difficult journey through the novel, gazing out from his moving viewpoint'. A 'pattern of consistency' is gradually perceived, yet 'at no time, however, can he have a total view of that journey' (Iser 1978a: 16). Hence it is that such dynamism of perspective opens up alternatives that we, at the start, did not consider. We may arrive at a 'totality emerging from interacting textual perspectives', but the really sustainable effect is that we formulate ourselves, 'and thus discover an inner world of which we had hitherto not been conscious' (Iser 1978a: 158). This therapeutic exercise does deepen our relationship with anything we read and it leads also to a heightened consciousness of how, in general, we piece together perceived details. This passage through anticipation and then retrospection marks the reading process, and leads to what seems to be a paradox: 'the reader is forced to reveal aspects of himself in order to experience a reality which is different to his own' (Iser 1978b: 281–2). Moreover, once we reread, the 'time sequence' of the narrative will be inevitably altered; we anticipate differently, and this variation is not a deterioration but rather the provision of an alternative set of perceptions. When we feel we have grasped how the work is structured and what implications are foremost, the situation is not exhausted. As we start to embellish 'our' interpretation, we also find ourselves challenged by 'new areas of indeterminacy' that intercede in the flow of construction (Iser 1978a: 287).

Iser's expansion of his ideas about the reader's role gravitated towards – as he terms it – 'literary anthropology', the search for a 'human' ingredient in perception. In the essays collected together in *The Fictive and the Imaginary: Charting Literary Anthropology* (1993a), he circles around at least two issues that mark out the importance of phenomenology: the element of 'play' where apparently disparate or irreconcilable elements may be contemplated without confluence and also the foundational status he accords to the Imaginary (in a Sartrean sense) and also the fictive in how we may conceive of reality. I cannot advance a reading of any artistic work that could be falsifiable or thoroughly disproved. An interpretation might be inadequate because it fails to take account of a sufficient range of textual details, or it might be outmoded because it fails to convince because time has moved on and audiences require different satisfactions: 'What counts is success, and not truth, and the former will always be endowed with the latter when it has been telling' (Iser 1993a: 89). It is the activity of explanation and defence that in effect creates one's readings. We hazard in 'play' in order to arrive at the figurative values of the most valuable texts and this entails a breaking away from 'code-governed applications'. Play is not a mere leisure additive, but rather an imperative so that conventions might be transcended and its customary signifiers 'split' into as yet unexplored expressiveness (Iser 1993a: 247–50). With 'play' comes 'performance'; just as, at the outset, the acting company do not fully know what the play might be that is in rehearsal, we best interact with the text in a rather unschematic and uncharted way. As such, 'performance' compensates for a lost mimesis, 'when both its connection to a closed world order and its intimate relation to the dignified object of representation were broken off' (Iser 1993a: 287). We play with a text so as to understand it (Iser 1993a: 250).

The conditions for drama need special consideration and Iser acknowledges that. A spectator is willingly controlled. The text is mediated by performance conditions and decisions, so the inspection of a dramatic text should be alert to the opportunities presented for such mediation. With this in mind, however realized by design and theatrical art, Rome and Alexandria are no precise locations; indeed, the efforts at even facsimile representation reveal only a facet of what the imagination will reach for. In the essays that make up *Prospecting: From Reader Response to Literary Anthropology* (1993b), Iser deals with the multiple facets of 'play' and 'performance'. If we are to be active respondents, then we must free ourselves from unduly mimetic assumptions, for 'play does not have to concern itself with what it stands for'. Indeed, increasingly through the immersion in such 'play', it 'does not have to picture anything outside itself'. Split into three stages or facets, this duality of recognizing the codes from where we begin in order to transcend them implies three uses or goals in any approach: a structural level, where we map the 'playground'; then a 'functional' one, where a preferred goal of the activity is explained; and then an 'interpretive' one that will eventually ask the more anthropological question as to why we need to play (Iser 1993b: 253–5).

We dig into a playtext because we desire more from theatre than restatement or easy cultural satisfaction. There are forces – ideological or political perhaps – that invite us to regard the world as monologic and so straightforward; what Iser calls 'doubling' is a recognition that dramatic action of the most profound kind involves us in doubt. We 'double back' on our first piecing together of plot recognition to comprehend that its events signal other and inaccessible factors that return to invalidate consumerist fantasies, where compensatory stories comfort us. Iser chooses *King Lear* and *Macbeth* to demonstrate such potential. *King Lear* invites us to regard the king's fated persuasion that all tends to 'the inevitability of endings' as a shortcut, as life goes on; in so doing, it outflanks an expected closure that he expects in dividing his kingdom and what lies beyond is a blasted heath and madness. Macbeth has (or inherits) a project of power and status, yet he learns what it is to be a powerless king (Iser 1993b: 246–7). Our 'decentered' fate involves us in searching for completion and a goal identified and grasped – yet the action involves a 'doubling' of meaning where words and grand gestures move towards troubling (yet enlightening) ambiguity. In *As You Like It*, for example, the two semiotic fields of Arden and Court, the pastoral and the socio-political, or engagement and desire, creatively overlap. As Jaques notes, the world is a 'stage' (2.7.139) and yet his settled melancholy displaces him not only from the court but also from the green world of Arden; the choric force that is also evident in Touchstone is an accentuation of Jaques's homelessness as the outsider may sense more than those intimately involved – but at a price. The masks assumed (Aliena and Ganymede) or the novelty of mutation that the courtly figures relish might show a resistance to polyphony and 'double meanings', yet through their own participation in staging themselves the mask becomes dangerously near to being the 'real'. In this, we similarly see the actor *and* the persona coexist: 'Outstripping the code testifies to the overpowering desire that breaks up the differentiation inherent in the code, whose distortion is proportionate to the genuineness of the passion to be communicated' (Iser 1993b: 108–10, 120). Would the passion exist without the projected fiction? Similarly, in his study of the history plays, *Staging Politics: The Lasting Impact of Shakespeare's Histories* (1993c), the fascination (and discussability) of the works depend on how much the historical record is left behind and its accepted narratives fail. Intention and status are only preliminaries to a realization that there is no stability and *telos* in the events portrayed. On the one hand, there is an attempt – perhaps from the source material of Hall or Holinshed – to conceptualize and domesticate, yet what we see occurring is 'reality as a happening without any bounds' (Iser 1993c: 192). Far from an immanent pattern, there is the potential to imagine worlds where we make our own fates – much like our own hermeneutic freedoms – and the presiding deity over this might be, from *Henry IV, Part 2*'s 'Induction',

> ... a pipe
> Blown by surmises, jealousies, conjectures,
> And of so easy and so plain a stop
> That the blunt monster with uncounted heads,
> The still-discordant wav'ring multitude,
> Can play upon it.
>
> INDUCTION, 15–20

To return to *Antony and Cleopatra* on Iser's and Jauss's terms means embracing any divide in semiotic fields. Most evidently, this is to do most characteristically with Rome and Alexandria, but also with what they introduce into the representation and what roles less heroic figures such as Enobarbus and Eros (among others) contribute. It is also to do with *what* we encounter when we buy the tickets for any performance of the play and what we are encouraged to anticipate. In Umberto Eco's terms, if we are to take our responses and the work seriously, we must identify the degree to which we are challenged by an 'open' text or one calculated to limit options, in a 'closed' text. For Eco, there is a defining difference between a work that offers possibilities 'within a given *field of relations*'. However much we relish the invitation to 'complete' the work and to do so in our own image, we should also recognize that we do this as an 'oriented insertion into something which always remains the world intended by the author' (Eco 1979: 62). A 'closed' text is code-driven to the extent that a reader can discern little more than the reassembly of known conventions. S/he might be enticed by how they are combined but there is no opportunity to question such conventions. Crucially, there is no metaphorical discovery, and Eco, in his essay 'The Semantics of Metaphor', puts forth an ambitious claim for figuration: that it can lead referential uses of language into new pastures: 'When faced with metaphor, we sense that it is turning into a vehicle of knowledge, and intuitively . . . we grasp its legitimacy', although we may not be able to demonstrate just what this 'additional knowledge' might be at first (Eco 1979: 87).

One obstacle to readerly immersion is to assign the causes for action to individual character and to known narrative forms. Shakespeare did consult Plutarch, but also the Countess of Pembroke's translation of Robert Garnier's *The Tragedy of Antony* (1590; reprinted 1592, 1595) and Samuel Daniel's *The Tragedy of Cleopatra* (1594; rev. 1599, 1607) and there is little doubt that the sad decline in their fortunes issued primarily from individual mischance. The clash between a tragic flaw and the need to supply pity for such weakness draws the reader/spectator to inspect the moral selves of the tragic heroes. Indeed, so much of the choric commentary does intensify our attention on them. There is, on the other hand, much more besides in the narrative.

The opening of the play has Philo voice a Roman perspective on the imperial lovers, wherein Antony's 'dotage . . . / O'erflows the measure' (1.1.1–2). We might suspect that the primary sense here indicated is that of behaviour beyond the mean, but there is a possibility that it connects with a legal stricture, too. For Antony, there may be 'beggary in the love that can be reckoned' (1.1.15). Without calculation or legal definition, there is doubt that ethics can be brought into the case. Rome might melt and, drawing on a partial allusion to Revelations 21:1, a new heaven and a new earth, could usher in a New Jerusalem where older perceptions are superseded. Cleopatra's own contribution is that she will 'set a bourn how far to be beloved' (1.1.16), a recognition that definition contributes to value. Philo remembers how Antony's 'heart' was once so great in battle that it 'burst / The buckles on his breast' (1.1.7–8). The metaphoric thread that plays with senses of definition itself is part of the train of connections that maintain a focus on what Antony and Cleopatra signify rather than what they could be said to *be*. When Eros unarms Antony in 4.14, it is part of the process whereby clouds cannot be kept in steady view (4.14.2–11) and Antony may be 'robbed' of his sword (4.14.23) to the point at which he 'cannot hold [a] visible shape' (4.14.14). The actors are and are not the parts they play, and Antony recognizes, on our behalf, that weighing (considering, estimating) is increasingly not part of the new world that he is experiencing. He answers Octavius in a poignant phrase during the high negotiations with Pompey where equivalence is at stake:

LEPIDUS   Be pleased to tell us –
    For this is from the present – how you take
    The offers we have sent you.
CAESAR   There's the point.
ANTONY
    Which do not be entreated to, but weigh
    What it is worth embraced.
CAESAR   And what may follow
    To try a larger fortune.

                                    2.6.29–34

The lure for Pompey is that if he accepts the present terms, it may play to his future advantage. Alternatively, this is a risky wager that could turn out (as it does) worthless. He has to remove pirates from the southern Mediterranean and 'send / Measures of wheat to Rome' (2.6.36–7). It is not obvious from the narrative just what he will obtain in return. At the next opportunity, Octavius takes advantage of Antony's absence to malign him in 'most narrow measure' (3.4.8), stinting of the praise and honour that should have been customary. Enobarbus catches at this shift of fortune, knowing full well that, in suffering, 'things outward / Do draw the inward quality after them' (3.13.32–3), and that Octavius knows 'all measures' about the wider world to the point at which he is 'full' (of what?) to answer Antony's 'emptiness' (3.13.36).

Iser's ideal reader is alert to looser semantic connections that would not normally fit thematic categories easily. We are led by semantic nuances the significance and application of which – to follow Jauss's emphases – come into and out of view as the audience are drawn to register them. The example of weight – gravity as well as worth – jostles references to the solidity of the body and legal definition. How they are configured becomes evident not through the application of straightforward semantics; by the fourth scene, the regular understanding of 'vacancy' is now associated with 'voluptuousness' (1.4.26). One scene later, and Cleopatra restores Antony to physicality by imagining him astride his horse: 'O happy horse, to bear the weight of Antony!' (1.5.22), a bridge to the 'sport' at the monument where gravity perhaps of all kinds is accentuated: 'How heavy weighs my lord! / Our strength is all gone into heaviness; / That makes the weight' (4.15.33–5). By the time that Dolabella attempts to console Cleopatra, it would be too literal-minded to judge it simply as sadness: 'Your loss is as yourself, great, and you bear it / As answering to the weight' (5.2.100–1) – but not as the Roman world could trace.

The most widely recognized advantage of Jauss's investigations lies in his influence in accounting for the slipperiness of certain critical terms and thus the historically relative assignation of value. A well-made play may appear on the critical horizon for reasons that may seem watertight – but only if we note how certain generations of cultural anxieties are addressed and considered relevant. A change in 'horizon' derives, from Jauss's account, once one hitherto neglected element of the text challenges an influential interpretation. One might here alight upon the recent emphases on Enobarbus's perspective and the contributions of once considered 'bit' parts, such as Eros and Charmian, or, indeed, Pompey and Lepidus, in a move away from a focus just on the tragic protagonists. Jauss's literary history prefers to follow a series of dislocations in the succession of re-evaluations that any work attracts: why does a work need to be adapted or truncated in order to satisfy its public? Why are gender and racial issues now so prominent in any reading of *Antony and Cleopatra*? As Paul de Man noticed, Jauss's sense of the 'aesthetic' needs careful handling, for it, too, has a history not just of a varied provision of pleasure or satisfaction, but also as a facet of perceptions of truth and veracity (de Man 2001: 326–7). For Jauss, at any one time, the difficulty in capturing the full meanings that can be culled from the signifier tend to be solved rather pre-emptively by claiming that we need only stress how certain 'horizons' have prompted certain master-readings; our investigations tend to halt there without isolating complexities of language. In terms, also, of literary history, there are some who are less in agreement with Jauss when it comes to valuing iconoclasm rather than a bold use of existing convention; as Terry Eagleton has it, for Jauss, 'the new is valuable in itself, and the normative inherently ossified' (Eagleton 2012: 92). One may respond, here, with noting that, for literary histories, that indeed is the point of the enterprise.

It is thus a complex matter even to identify just what the play *Antony and Cleopatra* might amount to, as it has appeared theatrically in varied forms and emphases. For Iser, the indeterminacies that inevitably emerge from any one perspective on a literary work is where the reader must begin work. It is not quite a matter of 'solving' or filling gaps in order to produce a fully unified authorial intention, as any Implied Reader becomes conscious that s/he is, in the last analysis, making it up as s/he goes along. We choose lines of consonance or dramatic value while being aware that there may be others. There is surely an invitation to search *Antony and Cleopatra* for binary oppositions derived from how there are differences along the Rome/Alexandria axis. The clash between duty and pleasure was usually asserted by time-consuming changes of scenery whereby one world stood alongside its opposite visually as well as verbally. That model is not quite sustainable, however, throughout any performance. Is it merely a matter of preferring one culture above the other? That first scene assertion of Antony's that Rome might 'in Tiber melt', dislodging the 'wide arch' of empire (1.1.34) as long as there may be a space for an alternative 'nobleness' (1.1.37), largely depends on how we perceive just how 'nobleness' might be summed up 'thus', and just what the 'space' he indicates might be (1.1.38, 35). Crucially, does it answer Philo's opening scepticism? When Enobarbus mistakes a regal approach at 1.2.79 for his master's, he is immediately answered by Charmian, 'Not he. The Queen' (1.2.80), and questions of identity are posed: where or what is Antony *now*?

Employing Iser's approach, there is much for the spectator to construct. Reading the play involves us in a basic judgement: how foolish (and so beyond redemption) might Antony be? Would *we* be seduced by an Alexandrian ease, and Cleopatra in particular? How far have our sympathies travelled since Philo's opening reductive view of their love? The full context for Enobarbus's enraptured description of their first meeting (2.2.201–50) also needs attention, for it is no soliloquy. Agrippa and Maecenas are there to be impressed and this dramatic grouping is Shakespeare's own invention, as North's translation is direct statement out of Plutarch. So it is that, despite himself, the battle-hardened Enobarbus is introduced to provide some level of ambiguity: not given to poetic fancy, he here indulges himself in – traditionally – the most memorable lines in the play. What is proposed as honourable or noble by some does not always add up in the midst of the action. The Soothsayer contrasts Antony's stature with Octavius's: on the one side, there is a 'daemon' that is 'noble, courageous, high unmatchable' (2.3.19), yet if Octavius were left out of account this would shine forth far more obviously. The calamity of the Actium engagement has Antony discover in himself 'a most unnoble swerving', his infatuation being the prime motive (3.11.50), and one of the results of this disgrace is Enobarbus's death (4.9.15–36).

Nobility clings to Antony, however, for Eros maintains the view that his master is still noble, even if he doubts that he can 'hold this visible shape' (4.14.14). Clouds take on shapes according to the vantage points of perceivers; in themselves, they approximate to 'indistinct' shapes 'as water is in water' (4.14.10–11), yet, increasingly in the narrative, nobility and honour come to the lips. The basic question to be resolved is: what do we see? Antony claims that he does 'not basely die' in Cleopatra's arms (after the haulage of his body up to the top of the monument), and she dubs him still as 'the noblest of men' (4.15.57, 61), and that may be a sincere opinion, yet by this point in the action we may well have come to accept her judgements in a wider context than any verbal extracts could illustrate. Cleopatra's closing determination to stage defiance and her own selfhood has a certain value and it frees her from the image in Rome that could denigrate her and Antony's memory. As a *persona*, she is 'marble-constant' about to perform 'a noble act' (5.2.239, 283), and Octavius comes to perceive her lifeless corpse alongside Charmian's, a mirror image of Eros's immolation alongside Antony's suicidal attempt. A noble end is not reserved just for the lovers; indeed, one could claim a degree of rather more honour in both Eros and Charmian voluntarily opting to die, Eros demonstrating more of a correct Roman fate than his master did.

With Iser's sense of the implied audience in mind, it would follow that there should be an emphasis on where the narrative 'fails' to complete the picture – that is, where we need to imagine beyond the given circumstances of the text. At an 'interpretive' level, we put something of ourselves into the frame once we have located an incremental sense of the work's structure and so the function (and focus) of our enquiries. It is here that the 'play' with the text comes into its own, for we deal with a dialectical 'doubling' of reactions where the very fact that the action is fictive carries with it a propositional status. Granted that there may be a number of points of entry is key: the charting of one course explores just one kind of unity, a path among others.

The text allows us to see displayed characters faced with doubts as to their national and personal selves, equivalent to any spectator's/reader's own self-exploration. Faced with the defiance in the face of fate exhibited by both Antony and Cleopatra, we either find their love ultimately demeaning or noble – or both. We can find the Roman world disquieting in its worldly success, but the degree to which this might be so is affected by other emphases we note that rides over single character studies; there are contributions to certain patterns that are shared by multiple characters. Consequently, any shape given the play (or novel) is a matter of perspective, a shape that is always composed of perceptions left behind and vestiges of this that help us get to grips with the onward movement of the narrative. In Iser's sense, reading is a matter of 'changing viewpoints, each one restricted in itself and so necessitating further perspectives' (Iser 1978a: 68). Eventually, one's personal engagement achieves a 'realization' of where that experience has led us, but the journey has been by valuing its aesthetic way of 'ideations' along the way that are destined to be forsaken once further experiences confront us. Iser's regular term for this is an indeterminacy produced by a perceived distinction between the interpretive roles of text and reader; it may be that in evaluating its aesthetic power we are drawn to appreciate interesting gaps or blanks rather than finding them blemishes. It might also account for the possibility that there may be a variable relationship with the same text when we reread it; we are different (older, in an alternative context, or now attentive for different objectives), so the text changes for us. This is especially so when we encounter the words and gestures in a variety of theatrical settings, where casting, design or even tempo of delivery start us off in new directions.

But is this to claim that the text as such does not exist in any objective way? The primary issue is now not what might our conclusions be, but where we might start. As we shall see in Chapter 3, there are vibrant strains of response theory that stress the formative influences of convention and presupposition: what seems novel or correct to us is derived from where we are placed – as Jauss reminds us – historically but also culturally. We shall encounter the theories of Stanley Fish more directly in the next chapter, but he figures at this point because of his challenge to Iser's approach and the debates promoted by the clash between them. Fish unpicks

Iser's notion of the indeterminacy of the text; its blanks and gaps occupy us to complete a reading. The unstable dialectic of whatever Rome might signify as opposed to Alexandria could be taken to be prompted by the text that pre-exists our thoughts about it, yet that there is a basic distinction is discerned from the text. Whatever 'Rome' is coloured in and constructed derives from that compass bearing. In his review of *The Act of Reading*, 'Why No One's Afraid of Wolfgang Iser', Fish distrusts the availability of his theory, how it seems to evade a prominent role in the inevitable clashes over whether our attention should be more drawn to textual or hermeneutic nuances (Fish 1981). If it is the case that the gaps in a text are created by the author or perceived by the reader (or director) does not often matter to Iser, as his emphasis is on the process leading on from that basis. Fish, though, returns us to what he sees as an oversight on Iser's part, whereby his dual perspective falls apart: one cannot combine in one process the status of text as an aesthetic object (one that is, ontologically speaking, an interpreter's creation) and also as embodied object (principally motivated by the writer). For Iser, there is a world that we can brush up against through the senses and the consistency of its existence: *Antony and Cleopatra* is transmitted to us via the sole authoritative version, the Folio text of 1623, and although most modern editions are reliant on Charlton Hinman's Norton facsimile (1968), there are still some variants due to editorial judgement thereafter. To note these minor differences is not to deny that there is a template upon which interpretation might work. Fish maintains that there are always prior constraints on this process, but that these are not textual but rather conventional. To prise interpretation away from the 'random or irresponsible', it is necessary to identify quite what these communal assumptions might be in constituting 'reality'. We will come to Fish's contribution to response theory in the next chapter, and his appearance at this point is not meant to focus on his own preconceptions. His reservations as to Iser's position are crucial, however, if we want to follow the line that there are textual constraints on his readings. Readers, Fish asserts, are always the 'product of the categories of understanding' that condition perception (Fish 1981: 11).

Let us return to *Antony and Cleopatra* for a while. If we would wish to explore the play's actual impact, then we would have to hold in abeyance some of the imperatives learnt from classroom rituals – not that they were beside the point, but that their use is apt to standardize a response. If we were simply the products of some inherited 'categories of understanding' or that our spectating habits issued from just one predominant tendency, then there would be an enhanced value in focusing on these categories rather than any distinctive use of them – by denial or significant modification. What Iser alerts us to is that we react dynamically throughout any performance; we form initial *gestalt* formations in our minds as to what the play is 'about', yet have these emended or supplemented as we proceed to follow the narrative. Emotionally, we may discover – despite warnings – a kernel of sympathy for the protagonists' passion that does not survive intact others' commentary or the disaster of Actium. By the time we get to Cleopatra's suicide, it is not as if we have forsaken past provisional opinions and so have them completely superseded. Indeed, we are prepared by the close of the action to contemplate a more 'open' set of possible perspectives on what might be an appropriate response. Octavius is a victor, but how do we evaluate the extent or justice of his eminence? We may instead agree with Cleopatra that a 'better life' might eventuate out of her 'desolation' and conclude that Caesar is 'paltry . . . / being . . . Fortune's knave' (5.2.1–3). That would introduce a dramatic contradiction, however, as we see Octavius disposing of Cleopatra's body in a perhaps clinical fashion, and his success is more likely down to calculation and not chance. Even the command that she is to be buried beside 'her Antony' allows for the possibility that her corpse cannot be accommodated in her own monument (5.2.357), and that her final resting place might be rather obscure, a diminution of her legacy that would smooth Octavius's future path to unquestioned supremacy. Any resolution of these contending perspectives is not to be found in the text; for Jauss, the emphasis at any one time is historically conditioned and for Iser, it is manufactured out of the text-reader/spectator interaction.

Jauss does allow, however, the validity of contemporary aesthetic judgements; what we now feel is no less valid than any records of past experience. Indeed, he opens up the prospect that there is no correct context in which to view; the past is always in the process of moving towards the future and at any one moment there are emergent and also residual impulses. For example, is Octavius (and the value systems he comes to figure) the victor narratively speaking? Does the play support Roman values? As I will explore further in Chapter 4, how we react with a degree of independence, and so resistance, to what is represented as uppermost at any play's conclusion needs careful inspection. For Iser, the navigations of dramatic viewing are not finally identified and patted into place by any closing disposition of characters or events. Thus, the display of female subjectivity ultimately survives her loss in the power games of portrayed history or patriarchal assumptions. We are not explicitly encouraged to put Cleopatra out of serious consideration, critically and creatively, because we may feel that that is not all that the play has to offer; there is always a serious supplement and complex reaction to Roman claims on our attention. Imperial duties ride alongside personal satisfactions, and Cleopatra (or Alexandria) are a necessary counterbalance to an Octavian future, that of empire and possession.[5]

We do not explore the conditions of existence because we cannot resolve our own version of identifying its origins, and whether a chicken or egg might claim precedence. In the debate staged in *Diacritics* by Rudolf E. Kuenzli in 1980, Iser was given an opportunity to extend and amplify his views in dialogue with Norman Holland, Wayne C. Booth and Stanley Fish, and he went on to be more detailed in his defence a year later (Iser 1980).[6] This clarification centres on the tripartite structure in question: 'The words of a text are given, the interpretation of the words is determinate, and the gaps between given element and/or interpretations are the indeterminacies' (Iser 1981: 83). Thus, there is the reader or spectator as a 'given' (and we can learn more about how such reading or viewing is placed in the world, such as when and how it takes place), a dictionary or denotative sense that we have to note in order to achieve a sphere of likelihood about sense (a determinate starting point), and then there is the move to interpret how certain segments might refer to each other (which are indeterminate). We become an 'implied reader' when we respond in an alert way to textual signals, but how we do that is never exhaustively prescribed by *what* we are reading. Indeed, Iser's approach is meant to be liberating yet not irresponsible. In his plea for the necessity for interpretation to be found in his essay, 'The Interplay between Creation and Interpretation', Iser outlines how he believes the two to be interdependent: 'creation is never pure creation but always dependent on given contexts within which it occurs and by which it is conditioned. Although creation exceeds existing limitations and even scandalizes hallowed conventions, it nevertheless is unable to free itself totally from what it outstrips ... Interpretation, in turn, is never pure cognition' (1984: 392–3). Where we may go thereafter – into matters of gender distinctions, ideology, racial reification – is not disabled by how we start our explorations.[7]

3

Literary Communities and Affective Experience

After the misadventures of *A Midsummer Night's Dream*, it proves a complex business for the lovers and the mechanicals to capture their experiences in words, yet some of the characters do try. Bottom's reawakening is not a completely pleasant experience, as the attempt to retrace his 'dream' evades verbal capture; his 'most rare vision' cannot be squared with the 'wit of man', for it involves a confusion of the senses. The most appropriate response would be poetic, that 'ballad' that he is going to request of Peter Quince, yet what even he might make of Bottom's recollections is not promising, for 'Bottom's Dream' 'hath no bottom' (4.1.213–15). In truth, lacking that unitary purpose, the memory merely fetches up floating images that defy conventional connections. It might be that the unlettered Bottom is unequal to the task that others might accomplish, yet he is not alone in finding their last night's experience beyond the norm. Theseus finds it 'more strange than true' what he gleans from the lovers about the wood's secrets, and associates lovers with madmen and poets, where it is the 'fantasies' of imagination that shape perception. The 'forms of things unknown' and 'airy nothing' only exist by dint of the writer's expressive talents. Hippolyta, however, is able to grant that, no matter how outlandish, there is 'great constancy' about their collective memory (5.1.2, 5, 15–16, 26). This search for the ineffable grants that dreams summon up deep responses, but these figurations are the best we can capture so as to come to terms (literally) with the imagination. Lysander realizes this when he tries to anticipate the travails of 'true love', and fears that it may offer only evanescent comforts like to 'the lightning in the collied night' and so is prey to the 'jaws of darkness' that bring 'bright things' to 'confusion' (1.1.134, 145, 148–9). If we delve beneath the conventional set of meanings, what do we discover? In this work, there are intervals of revelation that we strive to retain in experiential terms but, like dreams, cannot be gathered together with any accuracy in the accepted sense on recall.[1]

The perhaps awkward conclusion that we might reach is that we take shortcuts in assessing art's value if we similarly search for unified sense alone, or just one centre of gravity that coheres ideas of intention or overall meaning. While a plot provides a supply line, the real issue is of what? If there is a confluence of meaning and experience, then we have to move outside the words on the page. There is a parallel here with Freud's notion of 'Secondary Revision', whereby once we try to communicate our dreams, we are inescapably tempted to make sense of their details and so – in effect – falsify the nonsensical content. A censoring agency comes into play that supplies connections and an ostensible purpose: 'they seem to make sense, but this sense is . . . furthest from the real meaning of the dream . . . These are dreams that have already been interpreted, you might say, before we submit them to interpretation when we are awake' (Freud 1999: 320). The writer is indicated here: from this perspective, s/he may well be motivated by impulses not simply to tell a story. Indeed, the plot is not a 'pretext' as such but more an 'aftertext', a procedure whereby the deepest psychical material is dressed up in the representation. For the reader, the result is that we might be searching for a superficial causation, based on likelihoods derived from partial biographical evidence (including, where available, personal testimony) or a generalized sense of historical context, where the author is slotted into a hegemonic framework and we tend, therefore, to glide over any authentically individual choices or intuitions: 'the parts of the dream that appear clear to us are the ones where the secondary revision was able to accomplish something; in other parts, which seem confused, the powers of this ability failed' (Freud 1999: 327). For the theatregoer, there is the intervening work of the interpreters, director, or actors/designers that may generate their own attempt at coherence for us in the staging. Worthwhile drama, on the other hand, rarely operates on this basis: the even unfolding of the predestined narrative.

In alighting upon any set of themes in an artistic work, there is always a presumption that there is (somewhere) a unity that issues from *an* intention. Such a motivation might be an unconscious one or one barely acknowledged in any autobiographical testimony, but any reading is a 'making sense', where some traits are highlighted and some therefore left in the shade. Where *A Midsummer Night's Dream* is concerned, one might follow the contours of the plot to identify a number of themes (dream/reality, passion/control, or court contrasted with the world of the mechanicals and the forest near Athens, identity and metamorphosis). These preoccupations can be of greater or lesser significance given different lines of approach through different 'interpretive communities' or, in more subjective mode, one's own 'identity themes', but they can be identified through judiciously selected quotations. This perceptive analysis might indeed be a common factor or reference point for any number of theoretical approaches and across time; depending on where one might start from, one could juggle the details and emerge with subtly alternative results, but, as Norman Holland and David Bleich have it, these rather academic exercises can merely scratch the surface of what *feelings* are created by these dichotomies or clashes of perspective; it is more a matter of what we might do with such themes and how we give them creative value, both in the theatre and also in the study.

For example, there are in the play a cluster of references to 'eyes' (forty-one in all) and at least three in linked senses such as 'vision'. Even before their proper senses are scrambled in the green world of the forest,² the lovers are fixated on seeing correctly or clearly. The world of law and judgement Egeus and Theseus initially inhabit has the power to enforce certain perspectives on potentially illicit or distorted vision:

HERMIA
I would my father look'd but with my eyes.
THESEUS
Rather your eyes must with his judgement look.

1.1.56–7

The prelude to Lysander's fantasia on 'sympathy' (1.1.141–9) is Hermia's lament that 'hell' lies in choosing 'love by another's eyes' (1.1.140). One's eyes might indeed lead us in a 'spleen' of passion, but, like lightning in the night sky, it might afford just a satisfaction 'swift as a shadow' (1.1.146, 144). This is linked with Helena's envy of Hermia's eyes that seem 'lode-stars' in attracting Demetrius (1.1.183). Here eyes are a physical attribute, yet Helena also opines that 'form and dignity' might be created by perspective from a basis in 'things base and vile'. Blind Cupid is so because 'love looks not with the eyes, but with the mind' (1.1.232–4). To say that we might recognize how the 'mind' might create love is perhaps a rather superficial perception if we do not at the same time provide some personal involvement in that verdict. Certainly, in comic vein, Titania's delusions are due to the visual distortion caused by the juice laid in her eyes by Oberon when she is sleeping. He claims, though, that these produce 'hateful fantasies' (2.1.258)³ even if we claim them, as spectators, as comically absurd, as is Lysander's transferable passion that is now addressed to Helena. 'Love's richest book' is now written in Helena's eyes, allowing for the possibility that vision might be as much textual as immediately physical (2.2.121).

The challenge for any theatrical representation of the play is also an opportunity, for although we are told that the lovers might be able to regain their 'wonted sight' (3.2.369), can *we*? It is a regular strategy for those who do not know the play well that there are four candidates for an ending: Theseus's intervention just after the 'Bergomask' dance (5.1.348) that dismisses us all to bed, Puck's entry onto a bare stage that celebrates the 'darkness like a dream' where Hecate has a place (5.1.370, 378), the entry of the fairy world with the song and dance that – in some form – answers the grotesquerie of the 'Bergomask', and then, again on an empty stage, Puck's farewell to the play itself, dispelling the 'weak and idle theme' that inheres in a dream's visions as well as in performance (5.1.421). What is the 'wonted sight' to which we return? We may rest content with a sense that the play is comedic, yet that would be a rather broad-brush approach. The lovers are not sure that they are awake as dawn approaches and Helena utters a perhaps plaintive concern that Demetrius's affection for her might not be secure: 'I have found Demetrius, like a jewel, / Mine own, and not mine own' (4.1.190–1). It is also a salient detail that Demetrius's regard for her might be an infatuation activated by the juice squeezed on his eyelids by Oberon – and for which we see no antidote administered. Additionally, once we peer closely at Puck's closing invitation for an audience's tolerance, then there are signs that the 'shadows' with which we have been presented have been part of a fabric wherein we, as spectators, have 'slumbered' and have participated in a 'weak and idle theme'. Even though there is an invitation to awaken to a stronger and therefore more meaningful reality, the offer is voiced by one who *might* be 'an honest Puck' whose attempts *in the future* could be to 'scape the serpent's tongue'.

A Puck to be trusted is no automatic belief; as Robin Goodfellow or a hobgoblin, the sprite might be a domestic servant (he does carry a broom), but the mischief for which he is also known could be mendacious.[4] Often portrayed on stage as some sort of wilful imp, by these last speeches he is associated with graves that let loose the spirits of the departed at night, the fairy train that 'run / By the triple Hecate's team' and a tendency of 'following darkness like a dream' (5.1.377–8, 380). These are the ultimate associations for Puck, the ones with which we are left as the action comes to a close. No matter how merry and innocently comic his roles may have been earlier, he leaves us with a potentially sobering colouring lent to the unmasking of dramatic pretence and the return to zero-degree norms.[5] For both Jauss and Iser, one's responses are affected – if not guided – by external forces, either the text-in-history or the text itself. No one approach can yield a reliable array of meanings. For Holland and Bleich, one needs to leave the text further behind, for the process of meaning is more determined by a search for our deepest impulses that are brought to the fore by an encounter with fictive expression. Holland, principally in his *The Dynamics of Literary Response* (1968), *5 Readers Reading* (1975) and *Literature and the Brain* (2009), explored how the experiences derived from literature might be produced. Inevitably, he adopts psychoanalytic enquiries for his purposes, for they allow us to trace free associations and it is in literature that normative logic is most held at bay. Eventually, if one spends long enough playing with these linkages, one notes certain 'spreading activations' whereby the reader or spectator bypasses verbal capture and experiences sensations that are deeper and so personal, as regards both the author and ourselves (see Holland 2009: 187–210).

For Holland, we cannot help encounter a text but through our own predilections and preformed psychic structures and it is these processes on which he focuses. On the most available levels, one might assay generalized descriptions according to some quasi-philosophical template or, formalistically, by recourse to the enumeration of themes or patterns of verse, but this only scratches the surface of how we actually respond. A Puck in one production can hardly be equivalent to a Puck in another rendition due to altered production contexts, even if the chosen verbal texts in both instances are identical. The wood near Athens could be rendered as dark and forbidding as befits night-time or as some embracing bower; the fairies might be out of Arthur Rackham or Disney or, alternatively, subconscious emanations that challenge our capacity to domesticate them. A reader shares in the fantasy material in the text, but that is the start of a journey in which we might explore how we are affected by it, and how our approach filters a production's choices both accentually (in verbal terms) and visually by way of design. As far as drama is concerned, the physical situation encourages communal responses, but Holland aims to 'explain' how we immerse ourselves in fictions:

> The mental process embodied in the literary work somehow becomes a process inside its audience ... To say that, however, is simply to describe the phenomenon without explaining it. How does the fusion or merger of self and book take place? To what degree? ... Most important, why does this fusion or merger take place at all?
>
> HOLLAND 1968: 67

One could answer these questions by relating response to successful rhetorical or dramatic skill; the craftsman author artfully pulls the strings and we are transported thereby. If that is the preferred agenda, then we start and end with what Holland regards as a stance outside the work and a dealing in abstractions; by taking note of psychoanalytic techniques of therapy, though, we are less drawn to some 'central "point"' to the piece we are contemplating, but rather to some 'central fantasy or daydream' that lies below, but still organizes, any textual surface or accustomed meaning (Holland 1968: 7).

Returning to Freud's comprehension of how there is an urge to 'make sense' of dreams in the telling of them, we, too, believe we are reacting to literature meaningfully in a process of secondary revision. Just as we are split between our more 'sensible' self that seeks order in a dream, there is, however, still this underworld of apparent randomness. At our core we find a self that is 'repressed to the most primitive level of our being' under a 'sort of "rind" of higher ego functions', a state akin to the mind undergoing therapy (Holland 1968: 89). By 1975 and *5 Readers Reading*, Holland is bolder in his exploration of the dynamics of such interpretation. We do not constantly reinvent the wheel in a state of primitive innocence when we encounter new phenomena – literary or otherwise – for we develop a personal 'identity theme' that favours some details as significant and omits or downplays others. Explaining the text or our theatrical experience is thus not an 'objective analysis of the text' or night's entertainment but rather a path to the rediscovery of our own 'identity' revealed in the project of retelling to both ourselves and others. It is this transaction that should be the object of our critical attention, and the modulations and/or recastings of one's identity theme brings an analyst and the imaginative text to the same level: 'if we absorb literature like the rest of the outer world, through adaptations that protect gratification in terms of one particular identity theme, then we respond to statements about literature in the same way' (Holland 1975: 210). Gradually grouping personal habits of association we trace in certain forms of expression, Holland offers a model of how our identity might be recreated by reading freely. Shakespeare may, therefore, be a pretext for our own interpretive choices or compulsions. Thus, it matters little that my *Dream* does not directly engage with anybody else's; for Holland, there is the most basic set of meanings in a text (he does admit that), yet it is where these hints take us that is at issue – what we learn about our psychic life and our capacity to embrace pleasure.[6] Thereby, it is the creative exploitation of the text that takes the foreground.

Subjective criticism is an exercise that does not primarily supply knowledge about writing. Perhaps we might glean insights from witnessing how others delve into their intuitive readings of a work, yet these would be side effects. For Bleich, now in any case is the time of the 'subjective paradigm'. Drawing on T. S. Kuhn's sense of a paradigm shift, he notices how the Enlightenment history of empiricism might not be in the twentieth century tenable or worthwhile as a model for enquiry.[7] His *Subjective Criticism* (1978) adopts Kuhn's notions of a paradigm as designating a 'shared mental structure, a set of beliefs about reality' (Bleich 1978: 10). As a result, any resort to locating the 'real' or 'foundational' is in effect a human projection and it is locked into cultural position not by some self-evident objective status but by a 'negotiation among perceivers' (Bleich 1978: 20). The work of criticism, literary and other varieties, depends on a dialectical conversation, sometimes institutionalized and at times not, and, in this, the role of naming is key. Language is where elements of common understanding find their footing; for Bleich, this is a constant from childhood onwards, as *'representational thought'* gives us a sense of *'goal-directedness'*. The very separation of subject from object is guaranteed by syntax: 'This produces our capacity to view ourselves in terms of unconscious motives, in which we *assume* that all of our behaviour can become available only through language and thought' (Bleich 1978: 64), and, consequently, our own sense of agency is confirmed through language.

We therefore sense our own subjective centre through language and its continuing capacity to help us adapt to changed circumstances. On the one hand, an artist communicates in order to arrest our attention and not principally to inform us. The value of this indirection is that our imaginative capacities are brought into the mix in that we respond to the 'symbolization' of the aesthetic intention. No matter how exhaustive our closest readings might be, the process by which we evaluate and *experience* plot details is left untouched. We might not debate whether *A Midsummer Night's Dream* confronts any audience with multiple perspectives or with how we might be captive to imaginative representations; these themes are evident in most readings and productions of the play. For Bleich, however, the nub of the matter is how we interpret these features, how we 'resymbolize' these details in our sense of their motivation and in their explanation both to ourselves and also in negotiation with others. By these means, the real that is taken to lie outside of ourselves is actually created symbolically by us in our cognition. Calling upon Freud's view of great art (and Michelangelo's *Moses* in particular), Bleich sees a point at which normative language and conventions fail us, much as it does Bottom who cannot get to the 'bottom' of his dream.

Freud looks for an intention in Michelangelo's art as a means by which we can judge how its grasp on a perceiver might be so compelling: 'it can only be the artist's intention in so far as he has succeeded in expressing it in his work and conveying it to us, that grasps us so powerfully'. We are drawn, then to *interpret* it and we arrive at the point where we can only rely upon our intuitions, not the artist's, in this search. Indeed, Freud considers it superfluous to search for any definitive and conscious artistic intention.[8]

Stepping back from this hermeneutic position, we might be able to see how significant the academic seminar might be for Bleich, for it is pre-eminently in this pedagogical frame that we are invited to 'resymbolize' our comprehension of meaning and offer it up to negotiation. This was the cornerstone of his earlier text, *Readers and Feelings: An Introduction to Subjective Criticism* (1975), whose formula for an advanced model of negotiation (whereby we conclude the session with an alternative view of the text from that with which we started) is the optimum one. This bypasses, however, conventional empiricism, a learning experience where we learn 'how to do criticism': 'the true scope of feeling – or perhaps the true limitations of feeling – is essentially denied by intellectual reformulations' (Bleich 1975: 49). Preparing for any 'negotiation' – academic or otherwise – involves a looking within to discover just what we really feel about, and through, the text. This runs a risk of solipsism – the text is what we make of it, nothing more or less – yet this first step is subjected to the testing of one's own subjective opinion up against others'. There is a caveat at this point, though, in that any community of negotiators has to agree to share a common purpose before setting out. We then enter into this exercise by pinning our colours to the mast in 'response statements', written testimonies that become 'a symbolic presentation of self, a contribution to a pedagogical community, and an articulation of that part of our reading experience we think we can negotiate into knowledge' (Bleich 1978: 167). Our responses do not fully exist without our expressing them.

This could be due to the fact that the body – our instincts – determine how we rationalize. Drawing on the phenomenology of Maurice Merleau-Ponty, there are also certain other consequences that result from this shift in focus. In his *Phénoménologie de la Perception* (1945; Eng. trans. as *Phenomenology of Perception* 2012), the body in all of its materiality predates and stands apart from intellectualism and theory in its treatment and reception of indeterminacies and ambiguities. The intellect completes – consulting a principle of unity and integration – a 'whole' that is never 'there' sensorily. The result of this, according to Merleau-Ponty, is an ignorance of how the body functions as a necessary component of comprehension. This has valuable consequences for a theatrical experience, as 'speech does not translate a ready-made thought; rather, speech accomplishes thought'. When listening to any oratory, it as if we are under a spell, and when the speech ends, the spell is broken: 'It is then that thoughts about the speech or the text will be able to arise' (Merleau-Ponty 2012: 183, 185). Can one discover these so as to analyse them?

What Bleich stresses and Holland leaves largely out of account is the social element emerging out of negotiation. Holland's 'identity theme' cannot exist communally as it is linked to personal history and its psychological consequences. This manoeuvre in measuring response emphasizes, eventually, how we evaluate sociologically; the individual does not alone guarantee cognition. This is a concern of two further immensely influential commentators, Stanley Fish and Jonathan Culler, both of whom focus on the institutional and cultural grounds for arriving at aesthetic value. Fish's notion of 'interpretive communities' and Culler's sense of the need for 'literary competence' is usually the result of certain favoured nuances in experienced reading. We are never outside a preformed context. When they turn to transindividual end points that gain for subjectivity the pretension to 'knowledge', both show an awareness how vulnerable the creative critic/ interpreter might be to claims of escapism and baseless supposition.

In *Is There a Text in This Class?: The Authority of Interpretive Communities* (1980), Fish collects together a number of essays that circle around descriptions of the reading process and how we might be aware of what is at stake when we try to locate meaning *in* a text. One might be tempted to treat a literary statement or structure as located more or less securely in an original epoch, and by learning more and more about reading or responding habits at that time, we could limit likely meanings; yet this does not address the phenomenon of what a work *does,* or did, to the reader or indeed the spectator, and how the temporal process of semantic recognition might operate upon us – how we start out with preset assumptions and where and how those expectations are modified through the time of reception and within the process of making sense. One of Fish's clearest explanations of such a 'context' is in an essay from 1978, 'Normal Circumstances, Literal Language, Direct Speech Acts, the Ordinary, the Everyday, the Obvious, What Goes Without Saying, and Other Special Cases' (Fish 1978). Normal perception appears to be obvious and freed from a particular perspective, yet that is down to the fact that we are immersed in it: 'A sentence is never not in a context. We are never not in a situation … A set of interpretive assumptions is always in force. A sentence that seems to need no interpretation is already the product of one' (Fish 1978: 637). It may appear to be a proper and advantageous angle of approach to read Shakespeare with an eye for themes or the most memorable language, yet Fish notes how we are often educated into such appreciation. This is also true of the primacy of reading a script above spectating a performance of it; one seems to lend itself to the manufacture of a unified experience, yet performance is variegated and provides opportunities for improvisation and spectacular interruptions in flow. This is where – even for radical theatre – he believes that aesthetic value is assigned even to shock and estrangement because we are conditioned by the safer and more inoculated expectations of the 'interpretive community' we inhabit:

If the self is conceived of not as an independent entity but as a social construct whose operations are delimited by the systems of intelligibility that inform it, then the meanings it confers on texts are not its own but have their source in the interpretive community (or communities) of which it has a function.

FISH 1980: 335

The possibility that we may live through and in more than one of these 'communities' is telling and, furthermore, makes an investigation of 'communal' cognition complex and rewarding. It is also a means by which critical differences may be descried not by means of variance of character or individuality but rather with reference to basic inherited assumptions. Thus, Fish can lay claim both to a measure of 'subjectivity' when one interprets as we are not 'objective' when we interpret (how can we be?), since we are allowed to be original or even non-traditional only in that we recognize initial lines of sense and run against them. On the other hand, such a meaning could be 'objective' when one refers it back to the 'community' that has (already) helped establish criteria of intelligibility. It also leads to a sense that critical disagreement might be a tussle between rhetorics rather more than assemblies of fact. It is the patterns we conjure out of details that draws Fish's attention: 'the whole of critical activity [will be] an attempt on the part of one party to alter the beliefs of another so that the evidence cited by the first will be seen *as* evidence by the second' (from 'Demonstration vs. Persuasion', Fish 1980: 365). There is consequently the possibility for a dialectical progression; one might enter the lists prone to imagine *A Midsummer Night's Dream* as a comedy, and all roads might be seen to lead to that end, yet once there is doubt about the degree of that comfort one cannot easily return to it – and so on. Is the essence of our approach to the *Dream* reducible to separate, definable, themes? Does it end 'happily'?

In broader terms, this retroactive process can be evidenced in a more sociological sphere. Fish was at pains *not* to confine these communities to institutional pressures and conditioning. Within wider terms of reference, one cannot block from our consciousness the Stonewall movement, or populist movements, or, earlier, the Vietnam War or the dissemination of Freudian approaches to the individual. It is not, though, a simple matter of external influences; these modes of interpretation have their own momentum: 'The community ... is always engaged in doing work, the work of transforming the landscape into material for its own project; but that project is then itself transformed by the very work that it does' (from 'Change', Fish 1989: 150). Thus it is that not all models for knowledge are affected equally by climate change, say, or new technologies; what is more, the sense of a 'community' is not a bloc of static assumptions, but rather a cluster of interlocking tendencies, several of which might be more prominent (and explanatory) in the midst of external tides of agreement or influence, but not at the expense of those less consulted that could emerge in the future and change the momentum that produces a new template for seeing. Thus, any generic acceptance of what the 'comic' might be shades off into the satiric, the macabre or sinister – or the celebratory, regenerative and festive (see the description in Fish 1989: 150–60).

Jonathan Culler's concept of 'literary competence' seems quite similar, yet, on closer inspection, its foci are different. He first explored a linkage between a reader's imaginative engagement in reading and how it might be structured culturally in his radical reassessment of Flaubert's 'realism': *Flaubert: The Uses of Uncertainty* (1974), but his reading only attains a theoretical maturity in three studies that mark (personally and institutionally) the road from structuralism to deconstruction: *Structuralist Poetics: Structuralism, Linguistics and the Study of Literature* (1975), *The Pursuit of Signs: Semiotics, Literature, Deconstruction* (1981) and *On Deconstruction: Theory and Criticism After Structuralism* (1982). Whereas structuralism promoted the study of overarching codes and conventions that hemmed in and defined creation and response, the pursuit of semiotic decoding led to the disturbing realization that we are the plaything of language, a step that both Holland and Bleich could have taken but did not. It was in the conventions and linguistic governance of textual signs that consciousness was possible; figuration led and cognition followed. Digging up deconstructively the hold these predominant habits have upon us reverses the hierarchies imposed upon us by certain linguistic tropes and the lazy definitions of reality and nature that preside, often subconsciously, over our position in the world.

'Literary competence' is not just the result of copious reading, as it is also derived from a certain type of attention to the canon of traditional good taste. How one reads literature might develop through time – as we mature or in relation to historical change (revolutions, personal ill or good fortune, changes in the status and/or access to books) – yet there is a common bond or even law that is encouraged by institutional pressures.[9] Equivalent to a 'competence' in understanding statements in another foreign language, there is – to borrow a structuralist term – a knowledge of the distinctive rules and conventions of that language that adds up to a recognition of *langue*. Each individual effort at expression (an apparently single act or *parole*) can only be valued and comprehended once we have a generic knowledge that constitutes it as intelligible and possessing value. A growth in understanding of (and noting) literary potential in the reader and what is standard theatrical fare in the spectator marks out a 'competent' artist as well as an experienced responder. Culler comes nearest to a steady definition of such an experience in his *Structuralist Poetics*, placing the emphasis on a context that perhaps coercively is the sum of relevant 'knowledge and expectations of varying degrees of specificity' that we need to find any text fully intelligible (Culler 1975: 95). This is largely internalized to the point at which it is not a matter of consciousness or will.

The value in recognizing any culture's guiding modes of communication is one that can be of value outside of any literary process. As far as a specifically *literary* project of interpretation might be concerned, we get used to forms of mimetic reproduction, where a reflection of the normal constitutes the 'real' and, more and more rarefied, what might also count as a higher cultural product. These generalizations as to what might be valuable culturally also take their cue from literary tradition – the rather more generic codes that implicitly help us to understand what, for example, a stage comedy or absurdist drama should be. By such means, even the most unexpected departures from common sense in any fiction are 'naturalized' and can satisfy expectation.[10] Bundled up with these cultural predispositions are significant literary examples that have spelled out excellence and that are canonical.

By 1983 and his deepest encounter with deconstruction. Culler was moved to consider how any text might confront, and be deemed separate from, the preliminaries of expectation. Far from isolating 'an' experience derived from reading, he dwells on how one's grasp of how writing addresses us is never complete. We are left with 'stories of reading' that require the text to possess (at first) certain qualities and properties that set the process in motion and yield 'more precise and dramatic narratives as well as creating a possibility of learning that lets one celebrate great works' (Culler 1983: 82). As Elizabeth Freund has wittily grasped, the turn from structuralist codification to deconstructive scrutiny and doubt entailed a reversion from the reader as hero, 'successfully overcoming textual obstacles' on the path to 'self-realisation', to reader as victim, constantly 'manipulated by the uncanny text which puts in question his [*sic*] ill-starred quest for meaning' (Freund 1987: 88).

Perception that is relative to the personality of the individual is an ostensible theme of the *Dream* and it would seem that it does not require complex studies of response to bring it to light. One might, however, claim that the process of approaching and evaluating textual patterns is not easily predicted by carefully chosen extracts or episodes. For Holland and Bleich, this is where we start, not where we end, for the form of any representation is a signpost, not a destination. Indeed, Holland developed a line of analysis derived from the perception that literary form was ultimately a defence mechanism, riddled with projections, repressions and ironies (Holland 2009: 143–63). These slippery roads we are invited to take are really cover stories and it is our task to delve beneath both to unearth an author's deepest sense of her/himself and also ours. Bleich's sense of how we might 'resymbolize' our experience so as to render it comprehensible to ourselves and others involves an encounter with the patterns of a work, but then to make something of them that is dredged up from our own psychic history.

The most obvious distinction between Fish and Culler derives from their emphasizing different forms of 'communal' coercion. Culler is content to explore the stories we tell ourselves about how we make sense of new linguistic forms – how competences satisfy us and help us get to grips with them. Fish, on the other hand, concentrates on why such shared models take root, and his narratives of reading are parables of betrayal and reversal, how we need to revalue and even revision our first bases of understanding once we move through the work. In his two studies of seventeenth-century writing, while there may be traces of shared vision true of their historical provenance, the texts Fish chooses elude us and afford us experiences that are in themselves instructive. In his approach to Milton's *Paradise Lost, Surprised by Sin* (1967), the invitation to identify with the colourful Satan in the earlier books is strategic because we are meant, as we read further, to disabuse ourselves of this instinct and perceive a wider picture, of the white effulgence that is the divine, as we read on. We fall, as it were, and feel that abstract idea on our pulses. Slow to free ourselves from 'present circumstances' and our reasoning selves, we – as Adam and Eve realized too late – need only have a faith in God (Fish 1967: 244–5). The process of reading enacts what the text is attempting to illustrate. Similarly, in his *Self-Consuming Artifacts* (Fish 1972), we might wish for certainty out there in the text, but what if the reading experience proceeds so obliquely that it forms a dialectic that involves the reader in its variability and doubling back on itself? It might seem to convey some direct meanings, but readers experience the text 'beyond the aid that discursive or rational forms can offer' and so what we read 'becomes the vehicle of its own abandonment' (Fish 1972: 3). Thereby, one might more properly pose the question, not what does this sentence mean, but what does it do (see Fish 1970)?

To return to *A Midsummer Night's Dream* is to look intensively at the incommunicability of its action. By that, I do not claim that one cannot describe its plot in its barest terms; I can pinpoint what happens scene by scene, but that is not to indicate a meaning or experience, and that emerges from interpretation. Staging the play demands a deftness of touch that, throughout the play's theatrical history, has not been a clear priority. In a proscenium context, we could be content with a peep show glimpse of another world demarcated from our secure seat in the stalls. As Trevor R. Griffiths has traced in his edition, the earliest attempts at staging often suffered from a need to romanticize the 'green world' of imaginative release in order to highlight a schism between it and the strictures of a courtly existence (Griffiths 1996: 16–39). Bolstered by pictorial and operatic excess, thematic cuts had to be made so that the duration of the play was viable. Driven by the need for accuracy, Charles Kean's 1856 production (Princess's Theatre, London) included screens of the Acropolis, the Theatre of Dionysus and other hill features from around Athens. Herbert Beerbohm Tree's 1900 production has become notorious for rabbits gambolling around the lovers and the rediscovery of Felix Mendelssohn's overture and incidental music (1826). On the one hand, Victorian tastes demanded spectacle, so that even attempts at Grecian reconstruction were filtered through large-scale sets that summoned up the grandeur of neo-classicism. Harley Granville-Barker's reaction to this scenic excess (1914, Savoy Theatre, London) was to incorporate English folk songs, a full text, suggestive scenery (that did not demand time-consuming changes) and use of the forestage. Influenced by William Poel's work with the Elizabethan Stage Society (founded in 1895), Granville-Barker attempted to reproduce Shakespeare in what were understood to be Elizabethan staging conditions. This is a substitution of one preferred mimetic context for another, but it highlights a native tradition of local mores, a Britishness that links better with Puck than with Oberon.

These two poles of interpretation could be mixed, and in film or TV versions these are more normally expected. Max Reinhardt's 1935 Warner Brothers film exploited expressionist elements alongside detailed wood scenes – along with plenty of Mendelssohn and protracted ballet scenes. A more extensive denial of realism can be located in Peter Brook's white box version of 1970 (RSC, Stratford) that was circus ring, operating theatre and/or gymnasium. The fairies occupied a catwalk when not flying in on trapezes. There were spinning plates that Puck's wand passed to Oberon and Titania's bower was a profusion of scarlet feathers. Brook and his designer, Sally Jacobs, sought to provide a modern version of magic and traditional icons of fairyland and a green world that were untried and genuinely surprising. Brook summed up his own approach in his search for actors who had (or could learn) special circus and acrobatic skills 'because they made purely theatrical statements', a departure from '19th century conventions' (*Daily Telegraph*, 14 September 1970). It was a green world within us that mattered – as both Bleich and Holland favoured and explored.

This shock of departing from an attempt at capturing a past 'reality' and stressing how dramatic action reached out to the present enlists an audience's faith in illusion. There was a minor reference to this policy in Robert Lepage's 1992 Royal National Theatre production (Olivier stage) where Puck was played by a circus performer, Angela Laurier, whose gymnastic manoeuvres were often centre stage. The visual impact of the performance was matched by the design where a pool that occupied most of the stage area reflected a myriad of lighting effects and was surrounded by mudflats where most of the action concerning the lovers took place. As the night wore on, costumes got progressively soiled and even the front rows of the audience needed protection from splattering. Characters from the fairy and royal worlds punted across the water. By evading any directly mimetic opportunities, one's deep memories of mythic elements could emerge, initially summoned by the verse, but aided prominently by variegated theatricality. One strategy of gesturing to an unconscious world that emerged only fitfully in the Athenian scenes was by way of doubling Theseus with Oberon and Hippolyta with Titania – or (with more effort) the mechanicals with the fairies. The overlay of law and custom in the court was rooted in unacknowledged desires and urges explored in the wood near Athens. Thus the doubling of regal/fairy characters allowed for, ultimately, a more aware court, where the estranged Oberon and Hippolyta – victims of a purely dynastic arrangement at the start – might gain pleasurable self-knowledge in the wood and come to a form of intimacy at the play's close. This was most obviously attempted in Ron Daniels's RSC production from 1981, where the stony faces of Hippolyta (Juliet Stevenson) and Oberon (Mike Gwilym) in the first scene gave way to friendliness in Act 5 after they had experienced 'green' identities in the intervening scenes. There could be a variant of this in even narrower doubling, in Bill Alexander's 1986 RSC version, only Hippolyta inhabited an alter-ego of Titania. Indeed, the dream was predominantly hers, as there was an interlude of her encountering Bottom before the mechanicals' first rehearsal, and her being disrobed by fairies to become Titania. Janet McTeer was both excited and apprehensive at the transformation, yet the therapy seemed to work in that she finally acquiesced in the forced marriage into the Athenian court. However, there are aspects of dreams that challenge and confront the dreamer, and John Caird's 1989 production for the RSC decided to depart radically from the 'green world' template. His fairies were punk goths, recalcitrant offspring of concerned parents, and their habitat was a junkyard of discarded beds and bicycle wheels; even Mendelssohn was echoed only to render it discordant and updated in Ilona Sekacz's score – a reminder that the unconscious could be represented as composed of detritus and apparently random details.

The variety of methods and strategies that reveal engagement with a playtext demand a level of projection and animation that is encouraged by performance, but, as both Holland and Bleich testify, an authentic depth of meaning cannot reside simply from a superficial decoding of primary meanings and gestures, the meanings most traditionally associated with generic structures or that could be regarded as supporting a unity of conscious authorial conception. For Fish and Culler, in a community or by way of assent to what might be a 'competent' understanding of what we are meant to discover, certain texts make 'sense' accordingly so as to pre-empt – and thereby identify – any aberrant meanings. For Holland, the fantasy content that is shared by all those who interpret or adapt the playtext in a most straightforward direction – the surface verbal dream content – is where interpretation commences, for it is only when we progress towards a realization of our own 'identity theme' that an authentic encounter with the text can emerge. For Bleich, the text is far more indicative, even if our 'resymbolization' is a product of a willed dialectic with the script; we force ourselves out of the textual – or theatrical – world that is provided for us to reach for the emotional linkage that is really autobiographical in genesis. These accounts of how art affects us are collapsed into 'meaning'.

There are dangers here, for, as William Ray has noted, meaning could thereby become just 'a random subjective event triggered by an object beyond knowledge; criticism, an occulted process of narcissism and self-replication' (Ray 1984: 76). Explication of the text is abandoned early (too early?) in the operation of resymbolization. Holland's experiments with isolating how five readers reacted to the same text in *5 Readers Reading* were carefully chosen by the analyst to be various;

proceeding from the assumptions derived from ego psychology that, at base, we are individuals is perhaps worth exploring, but we run up against the proposition that Jonathan Culler prefers: that 'the individuality of the individual cannot function as a principle of explanation, for it is a complex cultural construct, a heterogeneous product rather than a unified cause' (Culler 1981: 53). Even though Bleich has a more sustained faith in textual existence, his belief in its pedagogical value, whereby 'response statements' possess a quasi-scientific status, itself relies on any negotiating group identifying a common aim. The progress towards consensus and so dialectical growth is likely to be imposed not deduced, and leads towards a form of objectivism, not necessarily of the text, but of how it is used as a springboard towards realization by certain generations or sectors of a responding public.[11] Further towards the sociological point of the spectrum, Culler and Fish gesture towards more communal paths towards interpretation, yet the need for there to be a definition of coexistent competences and how they therefore structure responses is a priority. Both 'literary competence' and 'interpretive communities' are terms that reward an elite experience of literary effects, yet drama, especially, thrives on various audiences and democratic points of access. I will deal with this consideration in Chapter 5 with reference to Shakespeare's location within a cultural public sphere. More significant for both theorists is to posit the need for exploring how these expectations infiltrate our psyches; we might think of a reading and its value for us as a personal matter, yet that is to avoid the consideration that many might think like us and for reasons that are ideological in origin. Culler was to modify his basic concept of 'competence' as mastery of the rules and conventions as a sort of diploma. Does he smuggle in a sense of the 'ideal reader', one who knows how to 'see' Shakespeare? If so, the response might be that such conventions are criteria of not 'ideal' but rather basic comprehensibility, a formulation he introduces in 1975: 'the ideal reader is, of course, a theoretical construct, perhaps best thought of as a representation of the central notion of acceptability' (Culler 1975: 124). What is 'acceptable', on the other hand, is conditioned by cultural typification, an added value that bolsters one's sense of cultural well-being. By 1981, he moves subtly away from these perhaps unwelcome connotations: 'notions of an ideal reader or super-reader ought to be avoided. To speak of an ideal reader is to forget that reading has a history' (Culler 1981: 51). What is more, there is always an appeal to norms so that communication might be judged to be accurate. Although this principle is akin to Fish's approach, there are salient differences: Fish draws our attention to the vitality of what leads on from a communal starting point, and he provides us with narratives of close attention to the swerves and dips with which such vigilance repays us. There is an evolution here in his thinking: an emphasis on literature 'in the reader' is gradually replaced by what stands outside the reading process or, rather, what predates it, yet it is the text that sparks our response, even if it is a journey of betrayal and wilful detour. It is predictable that Fish, therefore, comes to appreciate this tension more as stages in the process than as irreconcilable differences. There is an aesthetic experience, but then there are reflections upon it and dependent evaluation. Establishing 'acceptable' conventions is a prelude to noting its transgressions, and we may discover evidence of interesting or worthless novelty.

Fish is, however, switching attention from a determinacy in a text to a determinacy inferred from traditions of comprehensibility that give rise to understanding. Why might not the detailed and perceptive reading experience alter (or absolve itself from) an interpretive formula? In addition, as Culler points out, the model of the frail reader, apt to be misled again and again and who 'falls into the same traps again and again', entails the opposite from his more secure and 'competent' reader (Culler 1983: 66). Approaching a text new to us or a dramatic experience that takes the text on a journey we had not contemplated before is what we expect from the most effective drama. The stage history of *A Midsummer Night's Dream* illustrates no steady evolution but rather the sudden appearance of at times strange and perhaps alienating interventions that may at first be a challenge to comprehend with comfort. To bring such changes of perspective within our own community, or indeed competence, is to realize how potentially conservative the reliance on inherited formulae of response can be. Both Culler and Fish have, however, understood this and in their later works attempted to modify their more sociological models of motivation to recognize how change might be predicated on – at first – isolating pre-existing norms of understanding; in order to identify and so appreciate innovation, there has to be a sounding board by which it might be measured.[12] The success of this perception has its limits. In the most general level of description, one could draw some distinctions between communities that emerge out of drama schools, professional practitioners, school exam candidates, academic specialists – or, less pragmatically, Shakespeare enthusiasts. How distinct are these groups and are their competences to be assessed with one criterion of success in mind? Robert Scholes has made the valid point that without any steady reference point (the text?), we may find it difficult to evaluate the effectiveness or accuracy of any community's approach and thus how it might enlighten us about either the text in question or its cultural impact: 'it is like saying that bluejays and robins can never be seen by the same person because any person will be either in the bluejay community or the robin community and therefore will see only one or the other' (Scholes 1984: 176).[13] In critical practice, we must strive to look outside any 'educated' focus so that present values are borne in mind that are not limited only to material for examination preparation.

The more liberating aspect of Fish's theories rests in his models for affective stylistics, an emphasis on how we often find incompatible notions of unitary authorial purpose with a spectrum of experience that is open, contradictory and transgressive once we monitor closely what the aesthetic event *does to* us. Thus, a viable method of discovering what a play means might be to isolate themes that map entry into the playtext; illustrating their relevance is usually via the choice of relevant quotation or description of how character is revealed. In performance especially, however, the study of transhistorical themes and the characters that support such judgements do not determine very much. The impact of dreams and how they transform and/or enter into our thoughts do not lead to predictable results either for individuals in the study or specifically in the theatre. Two main examples might suffice: how do we come to know Puck and the brand of magic that he brings with him? How reassuring is the play's conclusion?

In Fish's kind of stylistics, Puck undergoes significant changes of identity – assuming that a 'Puck' has a human character in the first place. He is near to being a Robin Goodfellow in 2.1, a 'merry wanderer of the night' (2.1.43), yet at the same time he might be a hobgoblin under the sway of the devil (2.1.40) and a deceptive being, capable of transformation that offers mischief. Part of that devilment is to mistake Lysander for Demetrius in administering the 'love-juice' (3.2.89) and it might be merely 'sport' (3.2.161), yet there are aspects that lead one to associate him with darkness. He leads the lovers astray by enveloping them in 'drooping fog as black as Acheron' (3.2.357) amid night's ghosts and 'damnèd spirits' returning to their graves (3.2.382). There is a return to these associations in his closing lines; the screech-owl may wake the 'wretch that lies in woe / In remembrance of a shroud' (5.1.371–2). He may then represent the actor's predicament in his last words, gingerly awaiting the audience's reaction; if favourable, it works in favour of a theatrical togetherness, where there is a warm handshake, that dismisses the threat of the 'serpent's tongue' – a memory not only of an audience's hisses, but also of the serpent in Eden or the creature in Hermia's dream that is figured as a creature that 'ate [her] heart away' (2.2.148). The undecidability of how Puck operates in the narrative could be conceived as the point. Pre-emptive judgements as to how he may fit 'themes' short-circuits the interpretive process, because it is really the case in experiential terms that we receive complex signals as to what dreams, imagination or love might be that we have to complete. For example, the harshness of love and its randomness, its susceptibility to how we are attracted by merely sight of the intended, and how powerless we might be as mere mortals could only emerge if we took seriously the possibility that there was non-comic and non-pastoral potential in the text. As Fish demonstrates by tracing the mobility of his readers' responses, the altered states of where we might think we have grasped the text as a unity do not so much confuse (signifying perhaps that the writer's motivation was confused in itself) as lead us to revisit initial superficial assumptions. Given that the very process of gaining a sense of how any text signifies and how we feel about this journey contributes to the significance of the text, the focus might be more on how the alternations of worlds affects us: Athenian court/fairy world/mechanicals. Instead of dwelling on how 'themes' might lead us to any final synthesis, Fish would have us derive from our spectating or reading experience an event that moves us away from a stress on discursive or rational accounts and more towards a meaning that then is disclosed. It might well be that one could regard the broad rustic humour introduced by Bottom and his crew as light relief, a contrast to the hierarchies and appeal to law seen in Theseus/Oberon and Egeus's intervention in a world of desire, but the net effect of this humour could have us reflect upon the courts of Athens and that of the fairies in a different key. In 1.2, when we first encounter their rehearsing, the expectation that drama might merely consist of bombastic types such as lovers or tyrants, or that the untutored acting company cannot perceive the clash of effects promised by a 'most lamentable comedy' (1.2.11–12) has an enhanced resonance as the plot unfolds: the Shakespearean narrative does not involve us in such simple ordonnance and the eventual fruit of their preparations when they perform is lamentable, but only if we were to require 'straight' comedy or tragedy. Their simple motivations complement the lovers' turmoil and the enactment of their own tragic misunderstandings, perhaps painfully evinced by Helena at this point. As a flawed attempt at theatrical fiction, their lack of competence is overtaken by magic just as the emotions of the lovers is disordered by it, yet Puck's administering of 'love-in-idleness' is flawed too; he mistakes Lysander for Demetrius. By the time we expect a final achievement of successful union with Oberon's hymn to true and reciprocated love (5.1.395–416), there has been the exorcism of fated passion in the outrageous bathos of Pyramus and Thisbe's 'tragedy'. A neater conclusion would have allowed Oberon's words to usher us out of the venue, or Theseus's prediction of 'nightly revels and new jollity' (5.1.364), but we end with Puck, or, gradually, we might sense an actor playing him. What is the effect of the closing trope wherein he asks for our approbation 'if we be friends', allowing him to 'restore amends' (5.1.431–2)? If literature is most truly 'in the reader', then we cannot mute these appeals to our involvement, and the encouragement to find meaning in an individual's transcendence of tried and true conventions.

4

The Resistant Reader

Some preliminaries: there are strains of modern liberal theory that resist some of the assumptions that are likely to have underpinned earlier ideologies. In turn, it would follow that our own 'natural' motivations might not travel easily into the future. The focus of Marxist, post-colonial and feminist criticism lead us now to withhold easy assent to even the most deep-seated racist, chauvinist or supremacist impulses, and these resistant approaches merit separate consideration. The process of resisting expected or anticipated responses is still worth understanding in a more general sense. What happens to our reading or viewing once we find aspects of a Shakespeare play questionable? Might we simply conclude that that experience is not for us and we find other works by Shakespeare more to our taste?

If we were to take a step back, then we might find our starting point in how Wolfgang Iser noted this possibility. When investigating how hermeneutics was first identified as a distinct line of enquiry, he found an ally in the ideas of Friedrich Schleiermacher (1768–1834). In works such as *Hermeneutik und Kritik* (1838), he had investigated some of the details that led to 'self-reflective circularity', a syndrome whereby we find what we want to find in our interpretations of reality. Certain resemblances and correspondences – regarded as existing in a pure state external to ourselves – in fact just confirm our preconceptions rather than challenge them. We need, therefore, to take the risk of perceiving what seems to us 'unnaturally' – with effort and self-criticism:

> Speech uttered or written produces meaning or at least is intended to be meaningful, but meaning can no longer be grasped on the basis that both author and recipient participate in the truth-providing reason. Instead, the meaning of a sentence uttered by someone other than ourselves is basically something foreign, which poses the problem of how it is to be taken. More often than not, misunderstanding ensues.
>
> ISER 2000: 45

The very fact that we can now trace lines of congruence – perhaps in metaphors, word-chains or allusions – is not proof positive that these were intended by the writer in question – if this is any longer a deciding factor in the interpretive process. To this end, Schleiermacher asserted that we should aim to 'understand an author better than he understood himself'(Schleiermacher 1990: 191; the translation comes from Iser 1990: 46). The abiding question is, therefore, how may we reach for the 'foreign' in our processes of interpretation that does not simply promote randomness.

This balancing act is a particularly tenuous one where our theatre is concerned, for, even for subsidized companies, income from the box office is a condition of staging. There is always the temptation to dilute original ideas in order to be sufficiently consumerist, where the significance of any production is an easily comprehended event. To take the examples from the plays examined in this chapter: Shylock and Caliban often struggle against 'white' or Gentile prejudice, Coriolanus only seems to confirm an association between heroic behaviour and noble status, and Katherine is coerced into recognizing Petruchio as her lord in *The Taming of the Shrew*. If we encounter values with which we might disagree that are embodied within otherwise arrestingly dramatic encounters on stage, how are we to react? Do we silence our more ethical selves and just conclude that we might just go along for the ride because Shakespeare is Shakespeare the revered cultural icon? To some degree, there is always the encouragement to laugh or cry with the herd or use the play as a heritage piece in that we are commemorating the mores of a past age – or do we develop counter-readings? Resisting is difficult because the solidarity that is produced in what is marketed as 'entertainment' is designed – in most of our drama – to be easier to appreciate instinctively. On the surface, racial or gender stereotyping is alien to educated, liberal values and seems easy to identify; we would like to stand aside from inherited and posited expectations, but, at the same time, there is also a distrust of 'political correctness' that finds in the retention of such values a tone-deaf sobriety, or we might find, when we reflect on our more authentic responses, the vestiges of less welcome impulses. The spectrum of what could be amusing about, say, a stand-up comedian's repertoire might be harmfully constricted if we were in an immediate position to reject patter that we find we should have rejected when we were later to bring it to mind.

The central issue is one of involvement for, when one of an audience, there are mass identifications that might coerce a response from us. A more responsible and radical dramatic event, however, is a daring feat, for it runs the risk of avoiding some of the more available exercises of humour or saccharine sympathies. In Jacques Rancière's *The Emancipated Spectator* (2009), he tackles exactly this difficulty: how to bridge the gap between acceptability and the truly radical and where the instinctively palatable might be part of a more questioning approach, even to the point where it is denied. For this to take place, spectators must feel free to be critical in how they respond emotionally. Involved in this move, we have to accept an image or scenario that might be 'intolerable' or to be proof against the easy gesture on the road to a 'pensive' outcome. The reward is that the art we behold becomes directly dramatic and meaningful, carrying a charge that affects us in a deeper and longer-lasting fashion. For Rancière, there is an emphasis on embracing a challenge to that circular process whereby we are biased in appreciating, and so valuing more powerfully, what confirms our basic selves: 'for their part, artists do not wish to instruct the spectator . . . They simply wish to produce a form of consciousness, an intensity of feeling, an energy for action' (Rancière 2009: 14). In this, we should be made forcibly aware that any 'intolerable' portrayal of a victim or rank injustice can simply be typified: the 'victim', the 'prejudice', the 'senseless violence' or the easy projection of our sympathies that is evinced by such evil. We are safe in reacting to such available triggers, yet, for Rancière, there are deeper artistic aims – best grasped when we subject ourselves to the resources of several media that offer a 'pensiveness' that could derive from new connections between image and text that might not yet be hardened into formulae. Thus, the film or dramatic image is not parasitic on the word, but rather serves and extends it.

Psychologically, we become used to the pretence that there is a direct address from a text and ourselves; we strive to overcome any initial effort so as to render complex and perhaps historically distant expression familiar. Where that barrier is an ethical one and the text would seem to endorse unwelcome assumptions, we are compelled to read 'as if' we were other than ourselves. For Frantz Fanon, where his own racial origins were concerned, there was a perennial temptation to wear a white mask to disguise his own black skin. When growing up, the earliest lesson for any black reader is to disown her/his deepest impulses and assume that there is a universal 'human' content unrefracted by racial difference: 'the collective unconsciousness is not dependent on cerebral heredity; it is the result of . . . the unreflected imposition of a culture' (Fanon 1967: 191) As such, it can be altered – but how? For Fanon, his resistance would have to derive from a deliverance at the level of language; a Negro from the Antilles, for example, would have to accept that 'a man who has a language consequently possesses the world expressed by that language' (Fanon 1967: 18). In order to raise her/himself above an inferior status signalled by non-standard lexis, that set of powerful linguistic conventions would have to be embraced. The problem remains, however, concerning the stereotypes of race, a pre-existing division between the intuitive self and its cultural construction. Any Jew would have to contend with the prejudice characterizing her/him with a hook nose and financial avarice. A Black or Asian reader, in recognizing any 'colonized' status inevitably accruing to her/himself, would have to decide whether to play the colonizer's game and become assimilated or retain otherness in its own right. A female reader would have to discover an awareness of gendered understanding and to embrace it both culturally and psychologically.

The response to any text could be that we search for a 'human' response where the divisiveness of cultural specifics are considered not of account. A consequence of this 'utopian' position is that one can bury the instinctive reaction of one's 'other' self in order that one can reach successfully for this abstract self. Is this search one designed to capture an authentic response? Before feminist criticism was recognized as a viable strain of criticism, women readers were often placed in a rather schizophrenic context, where one's formative education led one to read as an honorary male: as Lee Edwards recognized, 'Imagining myself male, I attempted to create myself male. Although I knew the case was otherwise, it seemed I could do nothing to make this other critically real' (Edwards 1972: 226). Judith Fetterley in 1978 reminded us that it was not simply a matter of exclusion but, for women readers, one of *immasculation*, where the mask one was encouraged to wear was either a male one (a sympathy with male protagonists or a masculine pathology) or the 'utopian' option discussed above. This resulted in a position of 'powerlessness which derives from not seeing one's experience articulated, clarified, and legitimized in art, but more significantly, the powerlessness which results from the endless division of self against self, the consequence of the invocation to identify as male while being reminded that to be male – to be universal – is to be *not female*' (Fetterley 1978: xx). In subsequent returns to these issues, resistance has been brought out of the purely psychological sphere and the legitimacy of adaptation (and thus appropriation) clarified. Reading the text, as Patrocinio Schweickart advised, is often a conscious exercise of the choice to read it 'against itself', 'as it was *not* meant to be read' (Schweickart 1986: 50). The accuracy of the response is, therefore, not one to be read off against any original sense of reality or presiding context. On the contrary, it is a case of assessing its present impact and relevance while still maintaining a link to the source text, either by introducing a production of it (discursively or theatrically) that is meant to shock because it confronts past traditions of understanding or that exploits the text (which is still 'there' as a ghost) to go further than it was originally meant to and thereby to inhabit literature as a work now in its own right.

This is a matter of primary concern where female spectatorship is concerned, for the coercion of default occasions of forming *an* audience do not quite apply. There remain residues of patriarchal influence in any large-scale forum. How might this be resisted? For Judith Butler, the 'Right to Appear' is where the main contest might be, and this is not a simple head-count of biological difference, how many women as opposed to men in an audience; it is more accurately bringing into view female-centred concerns not as marginal gestures but rather as central and significant contributions to the portrayal of human identity in general. As already discussed in relation to speech act theory, 'performative' expression can also run alongside 'performative' behaviour: Butler takes seriously Simone de Beauvoir's phrase that 'one is not born, but rather *becomes* a woman'. As such, the word alone, 'female', seems to promise a practice that is determined and perhaps 'natural', yet Butler believes that the female itself is rather 'open to intervention and resignification', and that that is so in spite of the fact that 'the field of appearance is regulated by norms of recognition that are themselves hierarchical and exclusionary' (de Beauvoir 1949: 281; Butler 1999: 33, 2015: 38). Where Shakespeare is concerned, this is to run up against an instinctive barrier that claims rights in rendering an 'authentic' canon of taste. If so, any mix of genders or colourblind casting in the cast list is unacceptable, given original playing conditions.

The field has always been open for creative adaptation so as to redress the inherited imbalances of racism and patriarchy. One might mention the attempts to analyse the possible anti-Semitism of *The Merchant of Venice* in Arnold Wesker's *The Merchant* (later entitled *Shylock*, original production, Plymouth Theater, New York, 1977), where Shylock and Antonio are friends and join forces in concocting a 'nonsense' bond to help illuminate anti-Semitic prejudice,[1] or the eighty-minute monologue from Mark Leiren-Young as Shylock (in *Shylock*) at the Bard on the Beach in Vancouver (dir. John Juliani) in 1996, where there is no direct Gentile voice to intervene, or Rupert Goold's glitzy *The Merchant of Vegas* (RSC, 2011) with Patrick Stewart as Shylock who was as infected by the chase for financial security as everyone else. It could be argued that *The Tempest*, when first performed, dealt with the subjugation of a New World of primitive nature (see below), but this has been accentuated by Aimé Césaire in his *Une Tempête* (dir. Jean-Marie Serreau, Festival d'Hammamet, Tunis, 1969). As Laurence Porter has pointed out, Césaire does not have to adapt the Folio text too much to uncover its modern relevance (Porter 1995). The play makes it clear that Caliban ruled the island prior to the European incursion and, instead of returning to Milan at the play's conclusion, Prospero remains as a kind of colonial governor. Ariel and Caliban figure as the two distinct reactions of the subjected – the one compliant and who is rewarded, the other oppositional and left as miserable as when the action started. Césaire's mode of resistance is best represented by his *Discourse on Colonialism* (1972):

> I say that between colonization and civilization there is an infinite distance; that out of all the colonial expeditions that have been undertaken, out of all the colonial statutes that have been drawn up, out of all the memoranda that have

been dispatched by all the ministries, there could not come a single human value. First we must study how colonization works to decivilize the colonizer, to brutalize him in the true sense of the word, to degrade him, to awaken him to buried instincts, to covetousness, violence, race hatred, and moral relativism . . .

CÉSAIRE 1972: 2

One of the more subtle effects of portraying the colonizer as Prospera (Helen Mirren) in Julie Taymor's film of the play (2010) is a focus on the colonial power that is more effected by superior guile and subterfuge (as well as magic) than by physicality; Djimon Hounsu's towering presence gave the impression that he was led more by an ideological presumption than material inferiority.

Cross-gendered casting has been attempted with the aim at laying bare vestigial prejudices by Greg Doran for the RSC (2018) in his *Troilus and Cressida*, where the parts of Thersites, Aeneas, Agamemnon, Calchas and Ulysses were played by women; in Erica Whyman's *Romeo and Juliet* (RSC, 2019), where her Mercutio was cross-cast; and in Justin Audibert's *The Taming of the Shrew* (RSC, 2019), where the 'patriarchy' one expects of Gremio and Petruchio was transferred to female actors and – vice versa – the obedient acquiescence of Bianca and the angry counterpoint of Kate was given to males. Whether this inversion, however, actually gives birth to an escape from patriarchal culture might be questioned. Jill Dolan's alertness to the search for a 'feminine aesthetic' entails not just a reversal of roles within the residual system but a supplanting of that system itself (Dolan 2012: 83–98).

In these cases, close reading is not a prime or exclusive objective in one's approach. As Yves Bonnefoy sets as a necessary aim, there is a decisive distinction between criticism as an analytic game, the search for themes and modes, according to rules of unity and interrelatedness, and one where one's own lived experience realizes any author's marks on the page. In this latter encounter, we should not be afraid of finding reading as a 'form of writing' (Bonnefoy 1990: 795). Far from a feeling that one has betrayed the text, there is a truth in honouring its author by making something new out of it. In 'lifting one's eyes from the page' one is going further than analysis can ever accomplish: 'for what a poet hopes for from words is that they might open to that plenitude that descriptions and formulations cannot reach'. Bonnefoy does not advocate such a move as a deliberate ignoring of detail, for, while one needs to 'leave the text', it is as a consequence of having 'gone into and crossed through [the work] as well' (Bonnefoy 1990: 800, 802–3). Instead of stopping at the point of interpretational cogency, one needs to go further and contemplate contingency and feelings – and also a pervasive and accepted context where much goes without being said.

Let us take an example: in *The Merchant of Venice*, one of the unsuccessful suitors for Portia's hand is Morocco, who, confronted by the caskets, fails in choosing the one that contains her picture. And just in case we have temporarily lost sight of his blackness, his exit is greeted by Portia's 'A gentle riddance, – draw the curtains, go – / Let all of his complexion choose me so' (2.7.78–9). There is a temptation here to cut this couplet, to make things easier for the liberal viewer. As Portia is to carry, one supposes, the main romantic interest as the play progresses, this is an awkward moment because it uncovers an unpalatable racism. Is she to remain a favourite of the spectators despite this? Can she? This is inevitably linked in this play with anti-Semitism and instinctive homophobia; Shylock is the moneylender who is a (too) easy target, whose faith in the laws of Venice that might protect vulnerable minorities proves foolish, and several of the speeches of Solerino, Salerino, Gobbo and Gratiano would have to go too, given their insensitive chortling at Antonio's friendship with Bassanio. This poses the question as to where the centre of the play might be; the incorporation of gesture and design supplements any script and need not be congruent with it. In David Thacker's RSC production of 1993, the lines did not appear. At the other end of the spectrum, Derbhle Crotty's

Portia (in Trevor Nunn's Royal National Theatre version of 1999) was so taken with Morocco's poeticisms and appearance that she spat the lines out with tears in her eyes, the main tone being one of regret that he did not choose correctly and that, anyway, it would be extremely difficult for Belmont to admit such otherness. Making the most of what is the longest speech in the play, Chu Omambala's Morocco was undeniably attractive and not for typecasting with ridiculous intonations or a lack of gentility. When he reasons that

> I do in birth deserve her, and in fortunes,
> In graces, and in qualities of breeding:
> But more than these, in love I do deserve, . . .

2.7.33–5

it is surely feasible to regard these sentiments as true to the romantic ethos of much of the play, and, if class solidarity were to be consulted, he is more aristocratic than Bassanio, whose adventurous wooing of Portia is shored up by Antonio's financing, not an estate. Another strategy would be to cast a black Nerissa alongside a white Portia, as in John Caird's RSC production of 1984, where Frances Tomelty's Portia swept up her black maid (Josette Simon) to exit arm-in-arm, blithely unaware of the enormity of her prejudice. In the same year, Mark Lamos (Stratford, Ontario) brought this moment to confrontation, Domini Blythe's Portia made to feel deeply uncomfortable in the face of Caroline Clay's steady glare.

This 'resistance' is not an attempt at changing the original to 'fit', but it is a recognition that text conventions run along different lines from those we are offered in the theatre, where dissonance and the ironic gap between surface verbal sentiment and its delivery is always available. For Rancière, this potential contributes to a 'pensiveness' that accrues to 'a new status of the figure that conjoins two regimes of expression, without homogenizing them' (Rancière 2009: 122). At one and the same time, there exists a residual pressure to react in a traditional way that seems straightforward, even 'natural' to us, yet this is (thankfully) denied us in performance or, away from the theatre, in narratives that disallow easy immersion in character or emotion.

As far as *The Merchant of Venice*'s status as a comedy is concerned, it has become increasingly complex to accept its illiberal sentiments. Shylock's treatment and the dubious advantages of Belmont as opposed to Venetian conditions now should give one pause. Granted that the friendship of Antonio and Bassanio brings to the fore homoeroticism or the possibility of some virtues of male friendship, we might note the impossibility of its continuing beyond the play's action. Does Jessica successfully convert to become a Gentile wife? Could she? Do we just bypass these obstacles and strive to mitigate such textual details, especially in performance, or is it our aim to become the active 'creators' of our response that Rancière takes to be a sign of an emancipated experience? At first glance, Belmont – where the apparent resolution of the action takes place, leaving the awkwardness of Venice behind – is some romantic idyll, a landed fastness in contrast to what we have noted about the mercantilism and risk of Venice. On closer inspection, the two locations share several characteristics: both carry elements of risk – of freight on the open seas or a choice of caskets; the crucial elasticity of bonds and promises through legal process or via symbols of faithfulness (see Newman 1987). The most obvious source for Shakespeare's Act 5 is the tale from Day 4, Story 1 found in Ser Giovanni Fiorentino's *Il Pecorone* (1558). Portia is merely known through references to a Lady of Belmonte, and, although there is a misunderstanding about the ring pledge, it is not tinged with aspects of threat. Gianetto (Bassanio) is immediately troubled, yet all ends well (and easily so) – to the point where 'he 'began to enjoy the jest hugely'. This potential difference has a healing quality and the result is that, if anything, it 'multiplied the love' they share 'and they spent the rest of their lives in great joy and happiness' (Bullough 1957–75: 1:476). There is no final mention of the Antonio figure (Ansaldo) except to provide a neat equivalence in wedded joy when he marries a servant girl and as another guest in Belmont.

Shakespeare is himself, one could observe, a resistant reader. There are too many loose ends to allow us to enjoy a closing happiness unreservedly. This is evident from the onset of the last act where Jessica and Lorenzo open what seems to be a relief from the crisis of the trial scene of 4.1: vespertinal calm and a disarming lyricism. It would be as well if we were not too distracted by soft lighting and a less populated stage. The allusive range in their duet spans Troilus's fated love of the possibly faithless Cressida, Pyramus's death in trying to pursue his love for Thisbe, Dido's suicide at Aeneas's departure from Carthage and Medea's rejuvenation of her father Aeson (and as part of the process, the cutting of his throat), but more recognizably, bringing into the picture Jason's desertion of her (5.1.1–14). These dissonant allusions are not negligently thrown in; indeed, the culmination of this antiphonal section has Lorenzo introduce the possibility of Jessica's 'unthrift love' in the theft from her father and, in return, Jessica vowing to 'out-night' him in a persistent theme that he was full of 'vows of faith . . . / And ne'er a true one' by which he was guilty of 'stealing her soul'. (5.1.16, 23, 19–20). The pun – should one choose to find it – of 'stealing' (theft) and 'steeling' (strengthening) – is poignant. Jessica's last words occur some 230 lines before the play's conclusion and yet there is no plausible exit for her during that time: 'I am never merry when I hear sweet music' (5.1.69). The consequences of her 'conversion' have not been lost on many recent productions. In Bill Alexander's RSC version of 1987, he had them spaced from each other across the breadth of the whole stage and in a full glare, and in Polly Findlay's 2015 iteration for the RSC, Scarlett Brookes's Jessica was in tears throughout, refusing to be consoled by James Corrigan via Lorenzo's determination to dwell on harmony. Comic though the result of the ring badinage turns out to be if one is determined to find comic resolution, it suggests through to the end shades of faithlessness, and, with special intensity for Jessica, a reminder of that 'turquoise [ring]' that Shylock's wife, Leah, had given him when young and that Jessica had so thoughtlessly given away for a mere monkey (3.1.113–14). The provision of a (now deceased) wife for Shylock is a Shakespearean addition, as is the announcement – so near the end by just six lines – of Shylock's deed of gift (5.1.290–4) accompanied by no sign of how his daughter might regard this. Trevor Nunn's remedy for how this manna might be received (Royal National Theatre, 1999) was to have Jessica sing a verse from 'Eshet Chayil', a traditional Hebrew melody – a poignant echo of an earlier moment of intimacy between father and daughter when both sang a fuller version before burning candles placed by a photograph of Leah. For Polly Findlay, Antonio is as disconcerted by the arrangements in Belmont as he was mired in as much 'want-wit sadness' (1.1.6) at the start of the play, and he breaks off from following the wedding party in Act 5 as he is consumed with tearful disillusion. For Bill Alexander (1987), Jessica cannot ever become a Gentile wife, and this is marked in the closing tableau, where both she and Antonio tarry while Jessica's over-large crucifix falls from round her neck. It is Antonio who is first to pick it up and he holds it out of her reach as the lights dim.

What Nunn, Alexander and Findlay are accomplishing is to spectate actively for us, and, in so doing, they promote the active engagement that theatre provides, but it does not exhaust a spectator's participation. In Bonnefoy's sense, we need to become poets and/or painters over and above trained interpreters: 'the sense of a text can only begin to have meaning for us after the verification that consists – quite instinctively – in giving new life to its words with our memories or present experiments' (Bonnefoy 1990: 806). The apparent ease with which a romantic conclusion to the play places an emphasis on a 'good deed' in a 'naughty world' (5.1.91) or the retention of rank and status whereby 'nothing is good ... without respect' (5.1.99), as Portia regards the world, or a Belmont that is blessed with 'sweet harmony' (5.1.57), according to Lorenzo, is surely halted by a 'pensiveness' that runs congruent with other dramatic elements. For example, there is no warm welcome from Portia for Jessica and Lorenzo on her entrance;

indeed, they are included in her entrance after some thirty lines where they are clearly associated with her (other?) servants (5.1.118–21). Indeed, the dislocation between Jew and Christian is emphatically portrayed elsewhere in the action and often to the former's detriment, posing the question as to on what basis conversion could be possible?[2] No matter how resistant non-Romantic readings can be made to appear, it is still true that there is in all versions of performance true to the text a welter of racist comment on Judaism.[3] In order to arrive at these embedded possibilities we have to discern other figures in the carpet, or to force ourselves to do so. In attempting this, we might indeed find only strands of some redeeming features that we can rescue – but in complex dramatic texts the search is often worth it.

This is at the core of Bertolt Brecht's aim to 'alienate' audiences, whereby they are situated as critical spectators suddenly made aware that the everyday and habitual is created and can be made strange. His admiration for Chinese actors and artists rests on their capacity to stand outside of their immediate context (with its predictive range of gestures and senses) to allow us, even if temporarily, to stand outside of ours. In contrast, the 'bourgeois theatre' attempts to confirm a sense that there are eternal truths about humanity: 'Its representation of people is bound by the alleged "eternally human". Its story is arranged in such way as to create "universal" situations that allow Man with a capital M to express himself: man of every period and every colour' (Brecht 1974: 96–7). Brecht's own plays did battle with such generalized representation. When Brecht and his colleagues in the Berliner Ensemble, however, considered the issues represented in the first scene of *Coriolanus*, they stressed the engaged stance of spectating; loath to emend the inherited text, they considered how best to regard the action in radical terms. Mutinous and starving citizens confront the patricians' spokesperson, Menenius Agrippa, demanding a more equal distribution of corn during a famine. In answer to the assertion that grain is being hoarded, Agrippa responds with the telling of the Fable of the Belly, the upshot of this being that each body part has its role and the belly (figuring the senators) has the job of storing food initially as a preliminary stage in its equal distribution, leaving behind the chaff. There is little sign in the text as to how this fable is received. Caius Martius (later to be dubbed Coriolanus) enters and dismisses the citizens and their claims as undeserving of notice. Agrippa notes that there has been the appointment of five tribunes to speak on the citizens' behalf. Before any significant debate can take place, a messenger arrives to warn of the approach of warlike Volscians under Tullius Aufidius. Caius Martius is glad of this as it will distract those who might support civil unrest. Cowed by the external threat, the citizens 'steal away' (*s.d.*, 1.1.250), leaving the stage to just two tribunes who wonder how Caius Martius might act in defence of the state, especially as he is deeply *proud* and will have to serve under Cominius.

Without emending the received text, Brecht and his companions concentrate more on how to regard the script without preconception. Thus Coriolanus might not be the unproblematic 'hero' and the citizens simply an untutored mob. Their awkward responses to Agrippa's rhetoric could either be gullibility or comprehensible, given the imbalance of power between the patricians and citizens. In his *A Short Organum for the Theatre* (1949), Brecht's recipe for resisting the predominance of easier and traditional interpretations is not far from Rancière's search for 'pensiveness':

> Such images certainly demand a certain way of acting which will leave the spectator's intellect free and highly mobile. He has again and again to make what one might call hypothetical adjustments to our structure, by mentally switching off the motive forces of our society or by substituting others for them: a process which leads real conduct to acquire an element of 'unnaturalness', thus allowing the real motive forces to be shorn of their naturalness and become capable of manipulation.
>
> NO. 40 IN BRECHT 1974: 191

If one reads the whole action, Brecht notes how an overall strategy of divided sympathies confronts us: the abruptness of Coriolanus's invective against the citizens is in stark contrast with how Agrippa deals with them, and the perceptive comment by the First Citizen stands up well by Act 5: that his services to the state are to please his mother and in order to be 'partly proud' (1.1.38). It is also worth foregrounding that Coriolanus's entrance is prefaced by a complex patterning of approaches to an obviously agonizing famine. To this extent, Brecht's Shakespeare is a realist, tempering the offer to adopt a patrician view as ours by permitting multiple frames through which to judge how justified the citizens' objections could be. The *force majeure* that obliges a temporary union between the classes brought into view by the Volscians' aggression does not resolve the citizens' grievances; rather, it holds them in abeyance, and those disposed to feel that their insurrection is just comic can come to that conclusion, yet where else at this point might our sympathies be directed? ('A Study of Shakespeare's *Coriolanus*' in Brecht 1974: 258–9). The negligence that aids a caving in to 'the motive forces of our society' should be resisted. To be a citizen in Rome at that time was a sign that you were an 'enfranchised inhabitant' (2., *OED*) or one 'possessing civic rights and privileges, a burgess or freeman of a city' (1., *OED*), so the title of 'plebeian' is rather loosely applied, usually as a sign of patrician superiority.

The resistance towards which Brecht and his colleagues worked revolved around seeking that dissonance between stated sentiment and our appreciation of its displayed context, between what seems to be explicit and what we see being expressed. For Rancière, this could work on an emotional level – the 'intolerable' – and the more intellectual – the 'pensive'. For a resistant reading to be convincing to others, one has to note details often obscured by a sense of the 'natural' or accepted. To start with, one has to identify what, at any time, might constitute the tolerable conventions that pre-empt the interpretational process. At its most basic, this could be anti-

Semitic, chauvinist, racist or class-ridden and one might feel confident in rejecting these often unwelcome positions in theory and in isolation; once they are represented in a complex and rewarding dramatic frame, however, the 'tolerable' categories of genre or the normal come into question.

The class divisions that are announced in that first scene of *Coriolanus* are not as weighted towards the tragic hero – be it Caius Marcius or, as he becomes, Coriolanus – as a more straightforward template would have it. His own crisis of being is not only signalled by the change of name in 1.9, but the trial of assuming an alternative political status in becoming Consul.[4] As R. B. Parker discovered in work towards his Oxford edition, there is a 'special characteristic' of the action in that there are '"overdetermined" choices: decisions, that is, for which no motives are given, not because there are none but because too many, [and] conflicting emotional subtexts are possible' (Parker 1994: 30). This introduces deeper material if we take the route of placing the play in its original cultural context. It is generally agreed that the play is dated 1607–8, a time when there was a current of resistance abroad to limit James I's prerogative (see the City of London's determination to draft their own charter, a success finally concluded in 1608) and food riots in the Midlands about land enclosures and the conversion of arable land to pasture. In the wake of this, a severe winter of 1607–8 saw price fixing and hoarding. Given that the account in Sir Thomas North's translation of Plutarch's *The Lives of the Noble Grecians and Romans* was a principal source (trans. 1579) and outlined the citizens' main complaint as objections to usury, it is telling that Shakespeare's version is clear in assigning grain shortage as the contentious issue.[5] Conclusions, therefore, that Shakespeare's audience might be well disposed to the strong and anti-democratic commander do not tell the whole story.

While it is probable that any audience might be bombarded in performance with pejorative comments on plebeian mores, these issue solely from the patrician interest.[6] Brecht made it clear that some intervention might be licit, as stage directions were indicators included by editors and that were not directly attributable to Shakespeare. Hence it is that the Folio text exhibits some confusion in the direction at 3.1.182, where there is an entry of a *'rabble of Plebeians'*, altered by Peter Holland (to ensure consistency) in his Arden 3 edition to *'Citizens'* (Holland 2013: 282).[7] The Berliner Ensemble analysis stresses the potential fracture between statement and context; deep consideration of the verbal signs allows alternative readings that could be discovered in performance, engaging creative approaches and thus 'emancipated' spectatorship and directorial intervention. The crucial choice of emphasis from Brecht's perspective is between readings centred on a tragic individual, where Coriolanus emerges as a site of sympathy, and a more political approach where nobility and national identities are called into question. In Shakespeare's drama, whom does 'nobility' really serve, and how constitutive of individual identity are Roman or Volscian allegiances?[8]

Put in a wider frame of relevance, our responses to abstract naming are more susceptible to cultural influences. When we commence our spectating of any *Coriolanus*, it would be advantageous to disown whatever we might recognize at the start as 'nobility' or heroism. This would allow us to be more receptive to how the playtext presents us with its own constructions of tragic destiny. A case in point could be the portrayal of nobility. There are nobles and there are patricians, but do we observe them living up to their titles? Delving into the cultural moment of 1607–8, we would discover ample evidence to support a daring hypothesis that the steady state class divisions that motivate so much of the early action of the play may not have been shared instinctively by some of Shakespeare's first audiences.[9] In addition, as James L. Calderwood notes, both the plebeians and Coriolanus ultimately distrust linguistic effects. The latter's expressiveness is limited to an almost forensic and stereotyped style, a 'scientific language' that proves brittle when describing or when applied to changing events (Calderwood 1966). In short, the perspective that observes rather than sympathizes with the participants in the action is a viable judgement on audience response.

To be a 'noble' in this playtext is to obey in the main the conventional designation of the title as a marker of inherited status (see for example. 2.2.152, 2.3.236–43 (where Martius's noble lineage is detailed), 3.1.28, 3.1.56–7). However, increasingly, the tribunes are regarded as 'noble' according to citizens' opinions (3.1.271, 3.3.142). Threaded through these references nobility is associated with rather dubious qualities of 'carelessness' (2.2.14) or 'cunning' (4.1.9), and latterly it falls to Aufidius to define Coriolanus as 'noble' in a personal sphere, freed from Roman expectations (4.5.119, 4.7.28–9). This is also a quality that Aufidius discovers aside from the stirring acts of honour that, before the walls of Corioli, confer on Martius his new heroism. It could follow that conferred or inherited status could not be the whole story.

The distance from whatever we can discern to be an original semantic range of possibilities where Shakespeare's work is concerned can be reconciled with any modern perspective by treating his plays as for all time, indicating perennial truths and persistent themes. For Harold Bloom, this is largely because our present conceptions of the 'human' are grounded in a shared recognition of distinctiveness derived from Shakespeare who pre-eminently celebrated humanist individuality (Bloom 1998: especially 25–41). Indeed, 'can we conceive of ourselves without Shakespeare?' (Bloom 1998: 13). As there are so many reasons why we are as we are and so many factors therein, it would be extremely narrow to consult just literary sources for the answer to such a wide question, and, as response theory makes clear, literary allusions (assuming that we can treat our own sense of 'literature' as a universal) are just one element in interpretation. Cultures move and mutate and, as we shall consider in the next chapter, our return to any sense of origin is questionable as a casting vote when registering effect. In turning to Bloom's approach to works that have been resisted – instinctively and conceptually – within our own culture and often in its stage history, we find more to discuss than his proposition allows. A salient example is *The Taming of the Shrew*, which now demands a certain tact and inventiveness on the part of directors and other interpreters so as to make its perspectives on women, marriage and indeed also male behaviour acceptable. If this provokes resistance, then it is likely that other aspects of the play in performance can be brought into view.

The battle between Katherine and Petruchio is only one of the antagonisms in the action if one is also brought to appreciate the dramatic tussle with patriarchy that extends well beyond two characters. Bianca is imprisoned within her own gender stereotype, too; her first appearance allows her just four lines, expressing humble submission (1.1.80–4) in contrast to Katherine's independent wilfulness and outrage at Baptista's lack of regard for her: 'is it your will / To make a stale of me amongst these mates?' (1.1.57–8). There are allusions here to chess (the impasse of being in checkmate) and also a woman sold off and for hire such as a courtesan, a 'stale'. In contrast, it is, according to the patriarchal template, the younger daughter who has to wait for her independence, guaranteed by marriage, until the elder is off the father's hands. Social acceptability demands that her prime consideration is to be marriageable. From the Italian, her name suggests a purity derived from whiteness, but whether this is a restriction or indeed an accurate description is questionable. She shares her name with the woman associated with Cassio in *Othello*, and the fame of the notorious courtesan, Bianca Capello, was to be exploited in Middleton's *Women Beware Women* (1614–15). In 2.1, she enters with her hands bound and is confronted by Katherine, who quizzes her as to whether it is the eligible Hortensio or the rich old man Gremio she favours. In dramatic form, she is on several levels a 'bondmaid and a slave' (2.1.2) and it is likely that her passivity is a tactic, leading Katherine to realize that her 'silence flouts' the elder sister. The fate of being an old maid and 'dancing bare-foot' on Bianca's wedding day is a consequence of not just Baptista's preference for traditional family expectations but a whole society's cultural pressure. 'Leading apes in hell' instead of a husband to the altar is all too possible for her (2.1. 34). Bianca's beauty attracts both Hortensio and Lucentio in so sudden a fashion that it alludes to any number of romantic plotlines of instantaneous love, yet in 3.1 her management of her suitors gives the lie to her apparent innocence: 'I'll not be tied to hours nor 'pointed times, / But learn my lessons as I please myself' (3.1.19–20) – not quite the inclination of a 'Minerva', as Lucentio instantly wants her to be (1.1.84).

As part of an explanation for Katherine's 'shrewishness', the yoking together of the violent courtship by Petruchio on the one hand with the duplicities and complexities of the courtship of Bianca on the other casts light on both plotlines and the motivations therein. The latter is usually regarded as derived from George Gascoigne's *Supposes* (1566), whereas the former from any number of jest-book or fabliau tales based on the plotline of a battle of the sexes, where the tamer, often by unreasonable behaviour verging on the violent, wins the hand of the shrew (leaving us to wonder whether there is love in the arrangement or just acquiescence).[10] In the former, there is little psychological depth to the characterization, and Polynesta (the Bianca figure) is reified as the object of love interest and is only faintly represented; left pregnant two years previously by Erostrato, she has an additional motive to wed in order to protect her child, and so different (and more urgent) reasons to obey social convention so as to wed. Another – and more direct – source can be identified as *A Pleasant Conceited Historie, called The taming of a Shrew* (1594), an anonymous piece that exhibits a close resemblance to Shakespeare's play. When trying to assess how we can respond to the dual emphases of the Folio text, *A Shrew* offers an alternative that might have been a first draft or close influence at some point in the composition. Its more dominant narrative is the romantic pursuit of Bianca, and the taming contest is less obvious. More crucial by contrast to *The Shrew* is the use of the Induction material. Unlike Shakespeare's Sly, *A Shrew* has Sly stay on stage throughout (indeed he interjects occasionally) and he closes the action by waking up to be sent home by the Tapster to await an awkward confrontation with his wife. This Sly is confident that his 'dream' has been instructive: 'I know now how to tame a shrew, / I dreamt upon it all this night till now.' He returns home determined to tame his own wife 'And she anger me' (Hodgdon 2010: 394).[11] There is a neatness in closing the frame that commences with *The Shrew*'s drunken Sly duped by the Lord, huntsmen and players. After 2.1, this Sly does not reappear.

The temptation to incorporate this material in a production is strong; it reinforces the idea that Petruchio's overconfidence and harassment of Katherine has been a compensating projection of Sly's fear of being dominated by his wife. It is a 'play' and, on awakening, this Sly resembles the startled Bottom from *A Midsummer Night's Dream*, unable quite to comprehend his experience and to re-enter his normal world easily. It takes up the Lord's claim in *The Shrew* that the narrative might really just be 'a flatt'ring dream or worthless fancy' (Ind., l.43). Consequently, there is a perspective on *The Shrew*'s sexual politics that casts Katherine's closing acquiescence to Petruchio as a 'played' resolution, not to be regarded as part of the bundle of gendered comments otherwise available as Shakespeare's. When Katherine bows her head to Petruchio as '[my] lord, [my] king, [my] keeper' and offers her hands to be placed below his foot (5.2.147, 178), there is a further layer of ironic distancing involved: it is a ruse by which her husband might win his bet with Lucentio and Hortensio, and confirms their private understanding to stand together against prevailing social convention (see the co-operation in confusing Vincentio in 4.5 even if it could be resignation on Katherine's part).[12]

For Brecht, an awareness of how a dramatic work could be susceptible of an acquiescent reading, promoting a 'consumerist' pleasure that steers clear of any 'intolerable' tension, is necessary once we reinforce our instincts to resist any such 'satisfaction'. As we have seen in both *The Merchant of Venice* and *Coriolanus*, it might be more available to audiences to regard Marcius's exploits as simply heroic and the emotional blackmail at his mother's hands capable of evoking unproblematic tragic sympathy and, in Shylock's case, an emphasis on his vengeful 'otherness' as a way of excusing his rough treatment at Gentile hands. Indeed, any resistant reading might need to bear these invitations in mind. For Harold Bloom, invoking a 'human' universality, there is evident in Katherine's closing subservience the signs of a fortunate ending, more knowing than patriarchal assumptions permit in its recipe for female rule. The 'art of her own will' is 'considerably more refined than it was at the play's start' (Bloom 1998: 35). The overdetermined qualities in the speech, its gesturing towards appearance of compliance rather that the thing itself, might, against the surface rhetoric, be deciphered in her advice to '[seem] to be most which we indeed least are' (5.2.176) – yet this is not a full confrontation with patriarchy as much as a negotiation with it. Katherine's shrewish persona is not so evident and consequently she will still rock the boat of tradition, even if the arrangement serves a measure of enfranchisement.

That a compliant reading might appear as a 'correct' one is often identified by traditionalist interpreters as one that is supposed to hold together as a cohesive result of craft and universal relevance. Any evasion of Heritage Shakespeare is surely salutary, yet it might mean turning one's back prematurely – for some commentators – on the quest for original meaning. In E. D. Hirsch's terms, in studies such as *Validity of Interpretation* (1967) and *The Aims of Interpretation* (1976), there is an ethical dimension to hermeneutics, for we owe that original moment due attention; this involves investigations not merely reduced to a single author's intention (assuming we can truly know that) but also to a past awareness shared with her/his audience. The discovery of new probabilities about that moment changes our perspective and so we can reach for an 'objective' grasp of a world quite unlike our own and one that appears alien the more we force ourselves to inspect it on its own terms. The scare quotes around 'objectivity' are a concession to our sensitivity to the proposition that we can gain outright knowledge about any human creation, especially where the medium is a verbal one. For Hirsch, however, the search is worth it, for it is only through such delving that we can identify securely the 'meaning' of a text as opposed to the 'significance' subsequently ascribed to it by criticism and interpretation. If we do not keep this distinction in mind, then we confuse 'meaning with mental processes rather than with an object of those processes' (Hirsch 1967: 32). This separation keeps open the possibility that any response is open to correction by the discovery of more facts or linkages between facts that might subsequently come to light or which might have been initially ignored. What was once enacted provides (ultimately) an enduring meaning that might be expressed differently by succeeding generations or those which start from alternative standpoints, but they still form an object of enquiry, one that summons ingenuity as well as attempts at accuracy, but which can be said to exist outside of psychology and ideology. Thus, one's 'perception of a visible object like Coleridge's table or of a nonvisible object like a phoneme can vary greatly from occasion to occasion, and yet what [one] is conscious of is nevertheless the same table, the same phoneme' (Hirsch 1967: 37).[13] Hence it is that validity can be located in the ascertainable horizon of original implications. Hirsch's term for this operation is a grasp of the work's 'intrinsic genre': 'the type that determines the boundaries of an utterance as a whole' (Hirsch 1967: 89). This is not to be confused with the simple naming of literary genres or kinds; it resembles Iser's narratives of reading or experiencing, where, as we engage with literature, we are constantly attempting to make sense of it and this entails an openness to correction and modification: to arrive at full and therefore valid comprehension, we enter a 'validating, self-correcting process – an active positing of corrigible schemata which we test and modify in the very process of coming to understand an utterance' (Hirsch 1976: 33–4). Unlike Iser's sense of reading – and eventually differentiated from how it is derived from a sense of 'literary competence' or 'interpretive communities', Hirsch believes that we can be free of such cultural constraints by narrowing down the possibilities we encounter scene by scene, say, by relating them to a final unity that retrospectively we see as objectively there for all readers to recognize. What fits and conduces to a unity of purpose and achievement provides the casting vote.

This is why historical context is so important to the identification of such objectivity: if we can discount implications that just could not have been current for Shakespeare and his original audiences, then we are well on our way towards the recognition of valid reactions. The source for many prior assumptions – that helpfully excludes the eccentric or unduly personal – is the inherited sense of history. We learn 'types' of cognition (both as an accompaniment to our own contemporary predilections and as route-finders to the past) in that they are 'type ideas which derive from previous experience and can subsume later experience' (Hirsch 1967: 269). It is through this manoeuvre that we can come together as disciplinary professionals and, communally, converse with common (and lucid) rules of engagement. Although ambiguity is there to be dissipated or reduced, this does not mean that he regards artists as wedded to a clarity of expression alone; it is rather that he is in search of a principle that helps us adjudicate among the cluster of readings that emanate from complex texts.[14] Perspectives might change but that is because there is better evidence. For William Ray, this is where Hirsch's conservatism is most vulnerable, for 'new understanding is … frequently the result of scrutinizing the methods and criteria of knowledge independently of any evidence such methods may uncover' (Ray 1984: 102). Where do we establish hard-and-fast criteria, an empiricism that most may acknowledge?

Allied to this are issues that David Bleich feels are prominent when we interpret. The question he poses in his essay, 'What Literature is Ours?', is an urgent one for any humanistic education. (Bleich 2004). What are we taught, and so rely upon, in order to be better interpreters? If the answer is merely to trust our instincts more securely, then seminars are a form of encounter sessions, and perhaps none the worse for that. Bleich's answer to his own question is that little we read according to the syllabus starts out as 'ours', not just because we are removed from its inception by language and cultural assumptions, but rather that we are rarely encouraged to play any role in its creation (Bleich 2004: 311). The site of debate here is centred on what effect information about its original context might play, and therefore how may our own tutored responses react back onto the more instinctual selves in the playhouse.

It is often the case that it is a matter of from where one starts: we may find it attractive to rest on the assumption that *The Tempest* is a romance or comedy, but one could immediately find leverage in these generic descriptions and discover that any fortunate – or fantastic – ingredients in how matters work out are simultaneously a holiday from reality. This flow towards the super-real is tempting and one could name several productions that discover in Prospero's (?) island a wonderfully unspoilt Utopia – for Prospero and Miranda. To aid this, the action is shot through with songs and sounds; its early stage history contained a blind in its title to disguise the fact that, until well into the eighteenth century, it was not Shakespeare's text that drew the crowds but a heavily stylized and much-altered version by William Davenant and John Dryden: *The Tempest, or The Enchanted Island* (Duke's Company, Lincoln's Inn Fields, 1667). The fact that it drew an audience rather different from a Drury Lane or Covent Garden clientele is significant: Lincoln's Inn Fields was reputed more for 'entertainments' than legitimate drama. In 1674, Thomas Shadwell read the Davenant/Dryden text as operatic material (Duke's Company, Dorset Garden), an assumption that was echoed in stage design. The bookkeeper for the company, John Downes, summarized some of the efforts to entice an audience visually as well as phonically; one scene was played before a screen whereon there were painted '*Myriads* of *Ariel* Spirits', and another (presumably 3.3) depicting a table 'furnisht out with Fruits, Sweet meats, and all sort of Viands' (Downes 1708: 34–5). The full Folio text was not reintroduced into any repertory until 1749 and James Lacy's Drury Lane production, yet he could not resist a final-act appearance of a masque featuring Neptune and Amphitrite, imported from Shadwell.

The stage history of the play exhibits at least two salient features of interest where resistant readings might be concerned: a timidity until recently to treat seriously the 'subaltern', post-colonialist, possibilities in the portrayal of Caliban and Ariel, and to look beyond seductive spectacle so as to uncover Césaire's theses about the dynamics of colonialist power (see pp. 97–8). There are several reasons why music and a certain subservience might be the keynotes of the play in performance. Its first recorded performances were at court: a Revels account for 1611 confirms that one took place on 'Hallomas nyght' (1 November), and then another probably to entertain the guests at a wedding celebration of Princess Elizabeth to the Elector Palatine during the winter of 1612–13. On top of this, as one of the first works staged at the Blackfriars theatre, there was the temptation to seize hold of –and manipulate – the potential for theatrical wonder. The awkwardness of Caliban-as-grotesque seems not to fit unless, thematically, one might find the play's 'intrinsic genre' to be one wherein the 'savage' Other is introduced only for the action to transcend its claims on our attention.[15] Transfer the audience of the play to a 'world' context, on the other hand, and the narrative takes on a quite unexpected set of emphases from an Anglo-American perspective.[16]

Looking beyond Caliban's own form of servitude, one might as well bring into focus that of Ariel and Miranda. Ariel resists (perhaps on our behalf?) Prospero's determination to keep the spirit in thrall throughout the play. As early as 1.2, his obedience comes over as negotiated by Ariel, for there would seem to have been some understanding that, in return for the 'worthy service' wherein there was 'no grudge or grumblings', there was to be a remittance from servitude of a year, a time that is almost up (1.2.248–9). The succinct (moody?) responses to Prospero's commands are in the face of threats to 'peg' him in the 'knotty entrails' of an oak if he disobeys (1.2.295). There are more reminders of Ariel's desire for liberty (and Prospero's reluctance to grant it) at 1.2.499–501, 4.1.265–6, 5.1.4–6, 5.1.87 and then 5.1.95–6. Unlike as in Caliban's case, he is eventually enfranchised, but he is helping Prospero under sufferance – an ingredient highlighted in Sam Mendes's 1993 production for the RSC, wherein Simon Russell-Beale (whose Ariel had been more leaden-footed than borne on favourable currents of air) spat in Alec McCowen's face at the moment of his eventual release (5.1.318–20). John Peter (*Sunday Times*, 15 August 1993) regarded this as an 'aberration of taste', while Irving Wardle (*Independent on Sunday*, 15 August 1993) understood the effectiveness of the shock, yet thought that, ultimately, it was 'cheap' as it had no 'preparation and no consequences', yet there were those like Malcolm Rutherford (*Financial Times*, 13 August 1993) who felt that the gesture 'smack[ed] excessively of English literary criticism', a 'cerebral' detail that seemed misplaced.

There are, however, benefits, as Brecht perceived, in dwelling on dramatic impact and detail. Not all master/subject relationships in the play are aligned with the justice of Prospero's obvious superiority. That might have been the case if one simply concentrated on Stephano or Trinculo alongside Caliban. Miranda has been, indeed, cared for by Prospero on the island, yet she takes the first chance that presents itself to discover a new world (to her) with Ferdinand. A more sentimental writer would have included a few lines wherein the daughter confirmed an attachment to her father as she left with the royal party. One might look back on 1.2 where Prospero's lengthy exposition of their history is shot through with signs of Miranda's lack of rapt attention (1.2.78, 88, 106). Caliban is that 'thing of darkness' but a creature that Prospero has also to 'acknowledge' as his own (5.1.276–7). At the end of the play, with Ariel released to the winds and Prospero returned to Milan, the island will be once again his, one supposes, and he will be able to listen to the music of his environment unimpeded.

There are also some equivocal details supplied about Prospero and his actions. His return to Milan and his dukedom will be undertaken minus his magic and his books (see 5.1.54–7), and the closing Epilogue is a further divestment of his authority, where what strength he possesses is his own and that 'most faint' (2–3). The audience have to show him (or the actor representing him) 'indulgence' (20) which leaves us wondering whether there is here a show of repentance – and not just before the audience but *in persona* as one who is rueful about his past.

In visual and auditory terms, the play does exploit spectacle and music. We do not have quite a reliable guide as to how the play's music aids interpretation, but there is, in dramatic terms, a fascination produced that is not exclusively on Prospero. As Seth Lerer notes, attention is often drawn more to his attendants than on the one who gives them orders, more on the agents of the magic than the magician himself and where we see Miranda growing and looking to the future while her father declines and fears what is to come (Lerer 2018: 42).[17] This is to the fore when we look at the wedding masque Prospero devises for his daughter and Ferdinand. It ends in confusion apparently because – as was the case the first time round as Duke – Prospero was distracted, so wrapped up in the self-regard of his magic that he forgets the plot against his life. What is more, no matter how splendid the show may be, the text has it end depressingly; Prospero lets us know that from here on revels have come to an end (4.1.146), and there for all to note is the discord of an aborted masque destined (if it had run its course) in some variety of praise leading to unity of obedience to the presiding dignitary. A masque at court is one thing; taken out of that congenial setting, it may be open to question and parody. The gracefulness of the dance between the nymphs and reapers that Prospero calls into being ends 'heavily', with a sadness that might attach itself to reapers as signalling grim death and that could point to anti-pastoral. Stopping the clock, as it were, at autumn at the same time summons up the fruitfulness of that season, as well as a thoughtfulness about where the cycle might have led – to winter (see Gilman 1980; Orgel 1994: 43–9). We do not have to decree that every production has to exhibit darker hues or plaintive melodies; it is clear, however, that these possibilities are there and that there is a choice in the matter that does not lead to an aberration of taste.

Response theorists are in search of reactions to art that are truly instinctive, creative and, thereby, personal. While there is a recognition that gendered approaches are relevant when approaching *The Taming of the Shrew* and Marxist or post-colonial readings of *Coriolanus* or *The Merchant of Venice,* and both when encountering *The Tempest*, it is often the priority adopted by a deeper understanding of audience reactions to search for instincts that are more individual than usually covered by such theories. 'Essentialist' responses tend to be a pre-emptive force, even if they gather principles together so that their perceptions have a political leverage. The awkward tipping point is reached once we resist a predominant reading because we find it does not 'fit' our own deeper desires and we call upon our own memory or cultural need that may, or may not, be shared by others. This is more pronounced when, in order to enter into the emotional capital of any text, we have to adopt the mask worn so much more easily by those divided from us by gender, social class or race. In order to dismantle this closed circuit of understanding (that appears to us more obvious by education or tribal loyalty), we have to do some sort of violence to the text. Judith Fetterley's observation about the female reader or auditor of a male-authored text is that one has to forsake a belief in the 'human' that would cover all universals in the reception process: 'the first act of the feminist critic must be to become a resisting rather than an assenting reader and, by this refusal to assent, to begin the process of exorcising the male mind that has been implanted in us' (Fetterley 1978: xxii). That act of denial is often an act of will, as Terry Eagleton describes it in his *Walter Benjamin, or Towards a Revolutionary Criticism* (Eagleton 1981), operating in two stages: first, to isolate the 'rhetorical structures' that tend to deliver to us 'politically undesirable effects' and then to read against their grain, whereby such texts are to be 'violated, smelted down . . . and so reinscribed in new social practices' (Eagleton 1981: 113, 116–17). The most radical act is to adapt the text so that it 'reinscribes' the Shakespearean original as a new work altogether, alluding to while working against its source, but that is to engage with Shakespeare's text at one remove, a tactic that Brecht and his Berliner Ensemble colleagues often denied themselves in order to find the resistant thesis in the original.

What one may find is that the dramatic ironies of valuable drama escape soapbox rhetoric. Shylock is indeed vengeful and scheming, but the Gentiles are a main cause of that. Venetian law may be bent to suit power, as may oaths of faith and legal bonds. A martial hero without regard for the people disowns them but then betrays even his more personal heroic code in due course. Petruchio apparently tames the shrew, but what victory does he have? One extreme answer is that Katherine is *too* defeated; in Gale Edwards's 1992 production for the RSC, Josie Lawrence's arch bricolage of loyalty to Michael Siberry's Petruchio, a mixture of discordant registers, concluded with her broken and abject with her victor looking on in baffled despair. In Wilfred Leach's reading of the ending (Delacorte Theater, 1978), Meryl Streep hauled Raul Julia off, presumably for a victorious romp, yet at the curtain call she ignored the latter's invitation to exit stage left and marched off in the opposite direction. This Petruchio had learnt his own form of obedience and slouched off after her.

We may also question whether the most rewarding spectating or reading experiences are ever in response to a 'closed' text. In Iser's sense, there is often a series of implications provoked by the source that are *intended* to engage aware readers or spectators. This opening for a variety of perspectives allows for dissidence, a confrontation with a dialectical potential where what might have once been contemplated no longer has quite the coercive force that historicists require.[18] However, the status of original context is an alternative source for responsive alignment, and this will be considered in the next chapter.

5

Shakespeare and Public Responses

Our ability to encounter Shakespeare's words independently of our own preconceptions of culture and even politics is a complex matter. This is also highly developed whenever we join an audience for or watch any film version of his plays, where the access is always mediated – and not just by theatre and performance history but also by contemporary concerns. Response theories promote an attempt to discover values and effects that are more personal and unaided, always allowing for the realization that we may not be used to doing without these 'public' filters and/or we may be so acculturated that the route to authentic effects and aesthetic immersion just is not there in any pure state.

This chapter is in two sections. The first attempts to depict how Shakespeare's first audiences were constituted and also what conventions of playgoing helped form an early modern public sphere. I then move onto a consideration of how a consultation of the private/public divide might bear upon an approach to Shakespeare's work. The starting point is Jürgen Habermas's identification of the changing range of the public sphere in his *The Structural Transformation of the Public Sphere: An Inquiry into a Category of Bourgeois Society* (original in German, 1962). The study supports the contention that the growth of an awareness of public being tended to the development of a civil society in the eighteenth century, where the overbearing influence of church or centralized government was for a time suspended, and through the coffee house and a free press, among other public fora, public opinion was fostered and the freedoms that went with it. The German term for this sense of 'publicness' is *Öffentlichkeit*, which draws in connotations not so much of any physical public location as of an ideology or consciousness, the sense of belonging to a public and thereby being capable of comment on its affairs. Private commerce rather than any wide democratic franchise was the invisible cause, yet it promoted conversation without overt suppression, turning 'the reproduction of life into something transcending the confines of private domestic authority and becoming a zone of public interest, [and] that zone of administrative contact became "critical"... in the sense that it provoked the critical judgement of a public making use of its reason' (Habermas 1989: 24). It was also its fate to be short-lived, occupying a precious interval before religious, governmental and intense commercial competition occupied its space. There is always a danger that a mid-twentieth-century theory – and one that took as its *locus classicus* a situation that matured in the eighteenth century – might be misapplied to any earlier context. There is a strand of Habermas's (and his commentators') thinking that stretches the distinctions exploited when studying the Enlightenment to encompass a number of historical contexts.[1]

The term 'public sphere' does have a function in relation to the early modern period, even if its examples and effects are different from those indicated by Habermas. The most salient features of the 'publicity' that Shakespeare's drama inhabited derived from the nuance of religious observance and the sense of festival that erupted despite it. Humanism was bound up with new criteria for a variety of cultural phenomena, principally the search for basic human identity and rather less for the proper and sacred relationship between humans and God. The reliance on allegorical truths about behaviour was cast in doubt and there was focus on less predictable details about motivation and fate. For Peter Lake, when concentrating on the later years of Elizabeth I's reign, there appeared a 'gamut of print' and public performances that comprised executions, sermons, public show trials and disputations as well as plays. Suddenly, copious opinions and perspectives were available to the literate citizen and the shows of secular drama could attract the barely literate (Lake 2007). For Richard Cust, it was the time of the 'public man', who ravenously consumed tracts on civic humanist themes, the *vita activa* and modern (that is, not necessarily, classical) virtue. Over and above the pleas for unity and providential harmony in political discourse, the country became by the 1620s far harder to govern by the common clichés that bred obedience (Cust 2007).

Drama's role in this rapid intellectual 'turn' has its own ingredients, but it stems from a novel taste for public association in a secular framework. This sphere is not allied exclusively to the playhouse (see Doty and Gurnis 2018). One of the main channels for the advertising of plays was the posting of playbills on posts or other prominent sites. Each day prospective spectators would peruse the bills, often with little warning as to where and what was on offer.[2] To attract an audience to a play with no previous critical or stage history it was a necessity to provide a preview of the expected action of the narrative on the bills or, increasingly, on title pages of printed texts; hence also the need to engage audiences as early as possible, either by a prologue or a significant first scene where the appetite might be whetted and/or there was arresting spectacle. Print might deviate from any set theatrical version, but it could also capture just one night's happening or an ideal combination of a number of live events. Increasingly, it proved possible for printed forms of the plays to precede the viewing of performance, and the celebrity of authors was underpinned by an address to readers via specific prefaces or other forms of introit.[3]

Quite suddenly, one attended the playhouse because there was advance fame about its author and often because of the synopsis to be found in printed form in various media. This still does not quite manage to get to the root of the fascination felt by contemporary audiences and it is likely that it was not all derived from the poetry and shock of dissonance embedded in the narrative. Such a mixed collection of auditors is likely to be thrilled and charged with new-found energy. Anthony Dawson proposes that it was therapeutic for the nation as a whole: 'Elizabethan theatrical culture made the production and interpretation of images self-conscious and meta-theatrical, and so highlighted performance as a way of establishing and maintaining a national historical consciousness' (Dawson and Yachnin 2001: 174). When Macmorris, in *Henry V*, quails at Fluellen's hints at racial difference in the English forces, ready to defend his Irish heritage, he asks the profound question: 'What ish my nation?' (3.2.124); there is an attempt to answer it by portraying the victory at Agincourt as an English one, despite the contributions from a Scottish (Jamy), Welsh (Fluellen) and Irish (Macmorris) contingent. War leads to the formation of a common purpose.

Stephen Gosson (1554–1624) was no lover of the public theatres; indeed, his sense that this new form of entertainment was low and dissolute was expressed at some length in his *Schoole of Abuse: Containing a pleasant invective against Poets, Pipers, Players, Jesters and such-like Caterpillars of a commonwealth* (1579). There was little to choose between two-a-penny 'jesters' and poets or players (he did not make a distinction between actors and playwrights):

> Let us but shut uppe our eares to Poets, Pypers and Players, pull our feete back from resort to Theaters and turne away our eyes from beholding of vanitie, the greatest storme of abuse will be ouerblown and a faye path troden to amendment of life. Were not we so foolish to taste every drugge and buy every trifle, Players would shut in their shoppes and carry their trashe to some other Countrie.
>
> GOSSON 1579: 27

In his *Playes Confuted in Five Actions* (1582), his dazzled observation of theatre audiences found them 'a monster of many heades', composed in the main of 'Tailors, Tinkers, Cordwayners, Saylers, Olde Men, yong men, Women, Boyes, Girles, and such like' (Gosson 1582: D4.r). The challenge that the theatres presented to polite society was immediate and it seemed to come (from a Puritan position) from the most unproductive and impolite sectors of society. Idleness was the keynote of spectating, but there is a common thread that usually accompanies these descriptions: at a theatre, there was a public – or mob – that assumed a life of its own, and there were few other pastimes where there were similar threats to peace and politeness. Sir John Davies (1569–1626), an Inns of Court man and so-called wit, emphasized the uncharted variety of these gatherings in *c.* 1593:

> For as we see at all the play house dores,
> When ended is the play, the daunce and song,
> A thousand townsemen, gentlemen, and whores,
> Porters and serving-men together throng.
>
> DAVIES 1876: 1:18

Gentlemen were jostled by both 'townsemen' and 'whores'. For Samuel Rowlands, in 1600, the choices for a free afternoon contained a trip to the Globe 'to see a Play' or to 'visit *Shoreditch* for a bawdie house' (Rowlands 1600: 9). There are other related associations that the anti-theatrical lobby feared. The first can be exemplified by Henry Crosse, in his *Vertues Commonwealth* (1603), who saw impersonation of 'the infirmities of holy men' as common in the plays of the time, as was an extravagant sporting with the passions of 'the sovereigne majestie of the Realme', with the result that it became a 'May-game to all the beholders' (Crosse 1603: P3r). Ben Jonson's protracted and staged contest with audiences reveal much about the author himself, his determination to lift himself and his writings above a popular demand. His Prologue to *The Masque of Queenes Celebrated from the House of Fame* (1609) complimented his courtly audience and their 'quick eares' compared with the 'sluggish ones of *Porters*, and *Mechanicks*' who are addicted to 'at every act ... *narrations*' (Jonson 1609a: B2).[4] This disturbance of mimetic attention extended to metatextual features, obviously a component of an afternoon's entertainment. A Swiss visitor, Thomas Platter, was enthralled by a visit to the Globe to see *Julius Caesar*, at the conclusion of which, the cast – including supposedly the dead emperor – danced 'very marvellously and gracefully ... as is their wont' (Platter 1937: 166). Such jigs were not popular outside the playhouse; there came an order before Middlesex General Session of the Peace in October 1612 to suppress them at the Fortune as 'lewde' and attractive to 'cutt-purses', who mingled with departing crowds, 'many tymes causinge tumults and outrages'(Chambers 1923: 4:340–1).

While it is notoriously complex to arrive at a precise appraisal of audience behaviour at this time, investigations of this kind are helpful when coming to terms with a sense of Shakespeare's envisaged audience. The novelty of the experience can be contrasted instructively with how our expectations intercede when defining original theatrical encounters at the Globe/Blackfriars/Court. With no obvious pejorative intent, Gosson noted how engrossed (possibly for ill) audiences were in 'publike Theaters' when any 'notable shew' was presented, for they 'arise in their seates, & sit upright with delight and eagernesse to view it well' (Gosson 1598: C7v). Francis Bacon appreciated the fact that the behaviour of a crowd could be quite beneficial in the theatre and distinct from the meanings that accrue to individuals. Drawing his comparison with 'the Ancients', he could not consider public behaviour as deleterious, apt as it was to 'instruct the minds of men unto virtue'; 'wise men and great Philosophers, have accounted it, as the Archet, or musicall Bow of the Mind. And certainly it is most true ... *that the minds of men are more patent to affections, and impressions, Congregate than solitary*' (Bacon 1640: 2: 107). This 'public' life Bacon felt was beneficial, yet Shakespeare was as apt to have some episodes illustrate the uncontrollable mob instincts of mass attention; this bubbles under with Roman citizens in *Coriolanus*, the pusillanimous Londoners seduced by Richard III, and the incensed mob in *Julius Caesar* that puts paid to Cinna the Poet.

The basic contradiction as far as evidence of audience participation is concerned surrounds the degree of immersion and sympathy expected of an audience and whether this filtered into actual behaviour. The anonymous author (possibly John Webster) of *New Characters* (1615) included a section on 'An Excellent Actor' that portrayed a 'full Theater' drawn intently to the actor at the centre and lines of attention radiating out to the 'circumference of so many eares', such rapt attention leading to the assumption that 'what we see him personate, we think truly done before us' (Anon. 1615: M5v). Alternatively, for Ben Jonson, it would appear that, even in his early career, he sensed how complex the issue of audience attention or sympathy could be. His Valentine in *The Case is Alter'd* (written with Thomas Nashe, 1609) holds forth on his experiences in a 'Utopia' that is really England in disguise and, although there 'generally' were many who are 'very acceptive and apt to applaud any meritable worke', the most noticeable are those who do not: 'the rude barbarous crue, a people that have no braines, and yet grounded judgements, these will hisse any thing that mounts above their grounded capacities' (Jonson 1609b: A2v).

The need to approach audience response via a consideration of how it is placed within the expectations and impulses of specific senses of a 'public' is central to locating communal reactions to drama; as far as the effects of Shakespeare's work is included in any search for meanings (then and now), one has to come to terms with what playgoing was like and also what it signified and then contrast that with our own often unconscious recognition of what is appropriate about appearing or witnessing in public. The literature that this project has attracted is voluminous, but, as far as this study reaches, the focus should be on the search for the sociological status of drama – how it engaged with structures of class and how its emergence as a public art form disturbed and added to certain conventions of social interaction. We might be mindful of the networks of social interaction that occurred in the process of theatre going. Or, in other words, what non-theatrical implications were involved in spectating in a theatre?

Habermas's ideas were certainly conditioned by his own reflections on life in Federal Germany, and the consciousness of the Cold War divisions that beset a divided nation.[5] The reaching out to a hope of universal rights and reason (and its Utopian project) is explicable in terms of his own immediate context, but his identification of how people entered the public realm and its effects is still helpful when we look at early modern theatrical culture and it feeds into a rediscovery of how the Globe or Blackfriars world was so different from our own. Where Habermas – and subsequent commentators – see a public sphere as an abstract factor, derived from theatrical spaces while not being exclusively identified with them, one might wonder at the novelty of such secular public display, its fearless guying of authority figures and its capacity for depicting a world turned upside down where fools could see through the ceremonies of kings and the conferment of authority might be open to chance and random opportunity. As Lena Cowen Orlin has explained, this could emerge from a sense of licensed alternatives of vision, where one could properly get into focus the hitherto assumed or passed over, especially where the domestic (including the female gaze) could be brought to signify matters of public import: 'To take any phenomenon as a subject of display is to make an object of it. At the most basic level, it becomes an object of recognition.' Thus what mattered, say, in a private chamber – in the form of individual character formation or disclosure – could be of significant figurative power at large (Orlin 2015: 109). What Habermas recognized as a challenge to received opinion in the coffee houses of the Restoration and the eighteenth century was also exploited at an earlier date – to much anti-theatrical dismay – in the counterculture of the commentary of often itinerant actors and actor-managers. Literature carried a great responsibility in this:

> The bourgeois public's critical public debate took place in principle without regard to all preexisting social and political rank and in accord with universal rules. These rules, because they remained strictly external to the individuals as such, secured space for the development of these individuals' interiority by literary means.
>
> HABERMAS 1989: 54

As we have seen, the Shakespearean public was not a *bourgeois* spectatorship as such until the opportunity for dramatic experiment was grasped on moving to private auditoria. For a short time, there was a perceived freedom – analogous to Habermas's 'secured space' – where new voices could be heard.

Habermas's ideas, however, have not gone uncontested, for the abstract formulation of such a sphere excludes considerations of gender and race. If anything, his sense of 'public' does not translate well to the internet and simulated audiences (see Bohman 2004: 131–55). It also does not directly consider gendered status within the entry into 'public' sensibility (see Fraser 2014, McLaughlin 2004). These may be urgent recent considerations, yet – with the performative potential of being an 'audience' in mind – they may help illuminate the issues endemic to being a spectator of Shakespeare then as now.

What is often forgotten is that the very situation of public playhouses, especially in the 1590s, carried a number of connotations that permeated playgoing in the very act of travel to and behaviour at such sites. Walls and visible boundaries seem to demarcate and map difference, yet, as mental categories, they are the product of human imprints (of thought and often ideology) and such separation cannot prevent an osmosis that defies such assertions of distinctness and ordering. As Henri Lefebvre observes:

visible boundaries, such as walls or enclosures in general, give rise for their part to an appearance of separation between spaces where in fact what exists is an ambiguous continuity. The space of a room, bedroom, house or garden may be cut off in a sense from social space by barriers and walls, all the signs of private property, yet still remain fundamentally part of that space.

LEFEBVRE 1991: 87

This ambiguity was all the more pronounced by this form of theatre emerging so rapidly and gaining such popular assent. What we trace in much of the contemporary comment on these audiences is its insurgency on the one hand and yet its tolerance by the court on the other. As such, the event created its audience – or tried to – as spectators were not as yet accustomed to behave in any customary way. This is all the harder to define specifically, because the city itself was a forum for drama in an enlarged sense and where civic rituals were attractive *staged* happenings. Richard Mulcaster put it pithily when, on the day before her coronation in 1559, he observed Elizabeth's progress from the Tower to Westminster and regarded it as 'a stage wherein was shewed the wonderfull spectacle, of a noble hearted princesse toward her most loving people' (Mulcaster 1975: 16). Mulcaster does not enquire in any detail as to how authentic and thereby how linked the display of such sentiments may have been to an *unstaged* set of instincts. Stephen Greenblatt's view was that there was in abundance a form of 'social energy', born out of a perception of sudden change and freedom, of the permission of radical revisioning at war with prescription and repetition. This opportunity for a 'sustained collective improvisation' signals a spectator's acute inspection of surfaces and inherited roles (Greenblatt 1988: 14). The Illyria of *Twelfth Night*, the wood near Athens in *A Midsummer Night's Dream* alongside the forest near various locations in Northern Italy in *The Two Gentlemen of Verona* or Prospero's (and Caliban's) island in *The Tempest* might lead one to anticipate romance and escapist good fortune, yet within the confines of that 'wooden O' (Prologue, l.13) that the audience of *Henry V* was encouraged to sense from the off alteration and departures from the expectations of rehearsed and historical conventions were permissible and even expected. As the Prologue prompts us, it is in our power to envisage the 'swelling scene', where 'our imaginary forces' flesh out the represented vying for power in a 'little place' and 'within the girdle of these walls' of – initially – the Curtain theatre (Prol. 4, 18, 16, 19).[6] That psychological space affords us the power to imagine more than we have been accustomed to and, in return, reimagine the London locations – including the Inns of Court or the Court itself – as figurative sites.

Drawing on several relevant and deeply researched studies of London's cultural topography, we can identify salient features of early modern playgoing that are no longer prominent today. The first carries a sense of how significant the exact location of the venue for performance was: taking the risky journey across the Thames to the Globe (or earlier to the north of the city, to the Theatre or Curtain) meant voyaging outside the *polis* proper, as the Liberties designated a twilight zone of license and possible exile from the regulated rituals of the City itself. When Shakespeare and the King's Men turned their attention from 1609 to the second Blackfriars (the first had been vacated in 1584), there was an improvement in facilities (space for two galleries, a capacity for some artificial lighting and, backstage, more room for musicians who probably played between the acts and supplied a measure of mood music during the action). To meet increased costs and limitations on the size of audiences, the cost of seats rose appreciably, enough to narrow the range of those attending regularly.[7]

It is, therefore, complicated to arrive at a steady capture of *a* Shakespearean audience. Not only are there variegated constituencies within such gatherings but an attempt to confront initial class and gender as part of the dramatic experience. The attempt to analyse this hybridity is also part of the progress towards comprehending its theatrical energy.

Andrew Gurr's compendious survey of staging conditions gives us the most reliable range of testimonies, but always they are accompanied by warnings as to their general application, with due allowance as to whether there is anti-theatrical bias or vested forces that lent theatrical encouragement. His valuable analogy as to a distinction, as we may now view it, between an audience and a crowd is significant: the essence of a sporting occasion is that it is not predetermined, and offers itself to instantaneous and obvious responses from spectators who were watching the stage as well as others in the congregation as opposed to 'hidden armchair audiences in the dark of a modern auditorium' (Gurr 2009: 259). In Anthony B. Dawson and Paul Yachnin's ambitious set of dialogues on the subject of playgoing at this time, the unstable relationship between onlooker and actor is part of a fresh fascination provoked by Shakespeare and his contemporaries.[8] The very word 'participation' can be construed with crucially alternative emphases: it can be accurate when describing pantomimic expectations where audience reactions are conventionalized ('it's behind you . . .') but also on a sliding scale where one might move towards an immersion that is less expected and far harder to fathom. Robert Weimann has mapped this complication as an interfused continuity with a folk medieval heritage and a break from such tradition. The terms that are central to this approach are *locus* and *platea*, the one indicating a focus on a consistency that promotes the mimetic and narrative flow, perhaps via an upholding of fictional character that remains aloof from an audience, the other a more theatrical focus of attention, perhaps containing an irruption of low comedy or direct commentary – as Weimann later had it in 1992 – a setting that 'privileged not of what was represented . . . but of what was representing and who was represented', and thereby a resistance to the authority of the *locus* (Weimann 1992: 503–4). For Weimann, this not a mere relic, for it is a 'positive principle . . . at work, according to which the actor may achieve a specific degree of approach to, and dissociation from, the audience's world in order to move freely between the roles of subjectivity and objectivity, self-expression and representation' (Weimann 1978: 83).[9] This is a theatrical resource and its potency emerges from the valency of the symbolic and representational, far from any rigid spatial organization of the stage.[10] Weimann revisits this view of how early modern stagecraft evolved in its own way in his *Author's Pen and Actor's Voice*, in which he extends the scope of such interfusion mainly as concerns *Macbeth*, where we strive to identify with the tragic hero yet frequently encounter an incipient barrier compared with the apparently minor (yet thematically strident) Porter with his reservoir of diegetic gestures to contemporary, and thus more immediate, preoccupations (Weimann 2000: 180–208). One status is more inscribed within the narrative frame, the other appears exiguous and at a tangent to any narrative impetus. Another view is to explore the role of the actor's body, the very physicality of a stage presence that exists in its own sphere and that takes off from the textual script where there is often the attempt to create a consistent character.

We are not, instinctively, culturally and physically, approximate to Shakespeare's first audiences. While we may project onto Shakespeare compensating and now relevant commitments, that is no secure route back to any anticipated sense of stage or auditory. At its most basic, we have to imagine a quite alien cognition of time and place; as Matthew D. Wagner acknowledges, realistic theatre is based on a 'linearity of time' that actually carries an implicit proposition about causation and individual volition, but Shakespeare's dramatic actions allow the incursion of matters that lie outside present consciousness and their effects cannot always be captured within the limitations of stage duration: the gap between cause and effect can be ironic or gnomic (Wagner 2012: 119). Added to this is the consciousness of release from former constraints during the 'passage of the stage', either visible in terms of class and gender or invisible in terms of ideology and instinct. This is why Habermas's sense of how a 'public sphere' exists is of some cogency in reaching out to how the process of connection and sympathy emerged from any playtext. For the first time there is a court of artistic excellence that is down to what Jeffrey S. Doty names as an emergence of 'publicness', a condition of new self-confidence for hitherto largely invisible sectors of society (Doty 2017: especially 1–28).

In Darlene Farabee's investigation of how Shakespeare's stagecraft was attuned to audience manipulation, she commences her study by considering just how *Henry V* operates via its Chorus: at the beginning of the second act, in the imaginative passage to France and back again, there is a wry joke in assuring the spectators that sea-sickness will not result: 'We'll not offend one stomach with our play' (2.0.40, quoted in Farabee 2014: 1–3). At this point in the narrative, we, with Henry, must sit in Southampton, awaiting fair winds to France, and our patience may indeed be tried by the 'abuse of distance', through which the players will 'force' their play (2.0.32). The clear division of the action into five acts is signalled by the intervention of the Chorus, much as we are to see the trials and tribulations of Pericles chronicled by Gower before each act. The peregrinations of the Prince of Tyre seem to need a toleration on behalf of the anticipated audience:

> Thus time we waste, and long leagues make short,
> Sail seas in cockles, have and wish but for't,
> Making, to take our imagination
> From bourn to bourn, region to region
> By you being pardon'd, we commit no crime
> To use one language in each several clime
> Where our scene seems to live. I do beseech you
> To learn of me, who stand i'th'gaps to teach you
> The stages of our story.

4.4.1–9

Gower himself is an historical item as his *Confessio Amantis*, the most obvious source for Pericles' travels, was published in 1393, detailing the adventures of Apollonius of Tyre. Shakespeare, therefore, wants the audience to ignore more recent iterations in Lawrence Twine's prose version, *The Pattern of Painful Adventures*, dating from c. 1576, reprinted in 1607, and George Wilkins's *The Painful Adventures of Pericles* (1608).

The Chorus in *Henry V* is not as apologetic as on first inspection; as with Gower in *Pericles*, what is more prominently brought to mind is the writer's ingenuity. Jumping from location to location challenges – or activates – the imagination as the body is itself captive – in Southampton at this point (but actually in Bankside). We also are conjured to admire this skill as one body of auditors. The author may aspire to gain a 'muse of fire' (1.0.1) that could invent and manifest the events of the narration, yet, in stating that as his goal, he brings such imaginative capacity to our attention and suggests implicitly where our attention could be directed. Here we are in this 'cockpit', beholding some 'flat unraised spirits' representing historical events unfold on 'this unworthy scaffold' (1.0.11, 9, 10), yet just as the Chorus on the one hand might wish to transport us, on the other, he is anchoring us in the here and now. Gower might appear a venerable relic, yet, in his hands, we are requested at this moment to breathe life into ancient and all-but-forgotten lore.

Consistently, the Chorus tries to excite an active participation; we are urged to 'Follow! Follow!' and to 'Work, work' one's thoughts (3.0.17, 25) just before the narrative action of Act 3 at the 'stage' walls of Harfleur, where Henry prepares English troops, his 'friends' (3.1.1), to work as a collective. Their 'royal captain' surveys the subdued military on the eve of Agincourt, and finds them 'brothers, friends and countrymen', and we are told of his effect on their mood, with a 'largess universal' that emerges from 'his liberal eye' (4.0.29, 34, 43–4). Before the last act, 'we' are the carriers of Henry to Calais, and it is up to us to 'Grant him there'. In addition; it is up to us to realize our own 'quick forge and working-house of thought' to bring London citizens into the scene when Henry returns home (5.0.6–7, 23). In this process the London audience witnessing Henry in the stage-play world are the audience of 1599 and we are now too. This level of emotional attentiveness also brings alongside in an indivisible process the possibility of alert tracing of allusions to the world outside the 'wooden O'. One's emotional involvement is only one element in this diegetic encounter, since the Chorus also returns us to our present experience at the close of the oration prefacing Act 5; for we are reminded there not only of our having followed with rapidity Henry's ascent to heroic status, but we are asked to contemplate how his actions might be equivalent *in the present of first performance* to the Earl of Essex's anticipated return from Ireland, with 'rebellion broachèd on his sword' (5.0.32). This complex negotiation with spectatorial response is also present in the closing Choric statement (Epilogue), where there is a continuation of the threads pursued throughout: the *diminutio* that has it that the play is the product of an author's 'all-unable pen', where he is to be discovered 'mangling by starts' the story of Henry's greatness (Epilogue, 1, 4); the concession that it is unfeasible to do justice to the imaginative scope of the portrayed events, because he has had to proceed 'In little room confining mighty men' (Epilogue, 3); and, finally, that retreat from a grand imaginative vision to less reassuring and sustaining mundanity, where we cannot rest easy on Henry's glory but rather dwell on the historical reality of what was to happen under his son's governance – the loss of French gains and thus introducing, at this most glorious moment, a sense of its short-lived futility, and a reminder that this is a recursion to the *Henry VI* plays 'which oft our stage hath shown' (Epilogue, 13). Annabel Patterson has reminded us of how daring the Essex reference would have been, given his abortive attempt at usurpation in 1601 (Patterson 1989: 71–92). Of the two versions of the play (1598 and 1600), the Quarto of 1600 (with two further Quarto editions of 1608 and 1619) is usually regarded as the more conservative text, omitting all the Chorus insets (including the Epilogue), the hatching of the plot by the bishops to distract Henry from the reclamation of church property in 1.1, the Hostess's accusation that the rejection of Falstaff at the close of *King Henry IV, Part 2* had 'killed his heart' (2.1.87), much of the Harfleur siege and the dire threatening of its citizens, where Henry seems content to unloose 'hot and forcing violation' on virgins and infants (3.3.21), much of Henry's meditation on the anxieties of monarchy (4.1.255–80), and Burgundy's awkward reminder of the depredations of war wreaked on French families (5.2.31–67) that dilutes English triumphalism. It is not simply that the Quarto texts are less varied in their dual call on an audience's sympathy and, in contrast, its cool judgement; it is rather that they do not attempt to evince as much imaginative involvement via the Chorus's exhortations only to undercut it latterly.

Any audience for the Folio text has to be agile in its noting of mood changes. One's desire to discover a clear path through to the victory at Agincourt could have been satisfied by incorporating more of *The Famous Victories of Henry V*, although printed in 1598, probably staged a decade earlier. Although Shakespeare does introduce also aspects of Holinshed, there is much more direct acquaintance with the play, yet with some omissions or significant changes of emphasis. *The Famous Victories* is much preoccupied with Hal as the Prodigal, who is clearly a thief (*Henry IV, Part 1* stops short of this trait), and strikes the Lord Chief Justice. One conference with his father is enough to effect a radical change. Much of this prehistory to *Henry V* is glanced at in both parts of *Henry IV*. For Shakespeare, however, the clarity of the Prodigal narrative is jettisoned for less reassuring material, drawn on from hints in Holinshed in the main. The desperate ethical decisions that confront Henry are magnified; the judgement on his erstwhile friends at Southampton (also omitted in the 1598 Quarto) is much amplified. The taking of Harfleur and the strategy involved is only briefly mentioned in the earlier play, and the killing of the French prisoners is introduced for the first time by Shakespeare. What is foregrounded in performance is that the alertness requested by the Chorus extends also to a quandary as to the degree of identification we should allow ourselves with Henry. There is a series of decisions with which we are presented right from the first scene: we do not see Henry until after the debate between Ely and Canterbury in 1.1, where it is clerical *realpolitik* that will help sway the king towards his war away from an attention on seizing clerical lands, and, if this is accepted, then the overlong and detailed redundancy of Canterbury's explanation of the Salic Law (1.2.33–114) looks far less like a satisfactory illustration for the potential audience than rhetorical obfuscation. From the performance perspective, the threats uttered before Harfleur city gates are, on the surface, a prelude to acts of 'impious war', the kind of action that would be expected of the 'prince of fiends' (3.4.15, 16). Is this an ingredient of the king's character – otherwise obscured – that now surfaces, a determination to be the soldier at all costs? Or might we conclude finally that, once Harfleur submits, it was a show, serving the needs of ceremony that links with his later doubts as to how authentic regality might turn out to be (4.1.206–57)? Is it valueless 'ceremony'? On a more positive side, Henry does counsel Exeter that Harfleur's inhabitants should be used with 'mercy' once they have capitulated (3.4.54), but does that erase effectively the more protracted display earlier in the scene of potential rapine?

The play could qualify as a 'problem play' in its own right, in that action often confounds the need for a literal interpretation of words, and the consistent colouring of *a* mood is rare. What might appear to be a gentle jibe at French mispronunciation when we come upon Catherine and Alice at their English lesson (3.4) could have been calculated to arouse some native solidarity, yet the positioning of the scene just after the heavily demotic expressions of Fluellen and company narrows any gap between French incomprehension and an imperfect idiomatic delivery from the 'English'. It also begs the question as to why English has to be learnt – as value-added leisure in the French court, or because there is a perceived indemnity in helping Catherine assimilate in the event of an English victory? It has also become a safer bet to juggle with some of the less reassuring contrasts of the action as it unfolds.

Thus, it was usual to omit Burgundy's elegiac survey of a defeated nation right in the midst of the hurry to the fortunate and potentially romantic conclusion (5.2.31–67) or to obscure it as a weakness of the deservedly vanquished, obscuring the perception that soldiers 'nothing do but meditate on blood' (5.2.60) and what is left in Northern France but a panorama of ravaged families and infertile soil. Bell's acting edition of 1774 excised the language lesson of 3.4, the threats before the walls of Harfleur and Burgundy's otherwise sobering reminder of war's rapine, a move repeated (without comment) in the celebrated productions of William Macready (Covent Garden, 1819; revived in 1825 and 1837) and Charles Kean (Princess's Theatre, 1859). More significantly, the original text has Henry order the execution of the French prisoners as a result of his sorrow at Suffolk's death and the expediency of disposing of these expendable beings given a new French advance (4.6.32–8). There is no question that it is the murder of the boys by the baggage train that motivates this slaughter (which is announced by Fluellen at 4.7.1–4), which, given our more modern sensibilities, would have been less of a war crime and more comprehensible as a human impulse. Olivier's film version (1944) had his Fluellen commence the scene with a tableau of his holding a boy's body, while Kenneth Branagh in his 1989 film had Henry behold the bodies piled upon a cart, obscuring any reminder of his own questionable murders in the preceding scene as lines 5–9 are cut. Picking up on a manic mood manifested in his threats before Harfleur, Ron Daniels had his Henry (Michael Sheen – RSC, Stratford-upon-Avon, 1997) – causing visible anxiety in his men – show no reaction at an order that was presented as cold-blooded and vicious. Matthew Warchus (RST, 1994) had Iain Glen, as his Henry, seize Pistol's sword in order to slit Le Fer's throat himself. Calling on an immediate political preoccupation – Essex's Irish campaign – Joel B. Altman highlights the prevalence of anticipated as well as represented violence suggested by the text: where there is a strategic 'amplification ambiguously reassuring and threatening, which offers up images of rational accessibility juxtaposed with those of imperial closure' (Altman 1991: 24). We deliberately cannot *know* the king. This is why, using the famous gestalt outline whereby one cannot see both a duck and a rabbit simultaneously in the same image, Norman Rabkin discovers a profound ambiguity in the action, 'requiring that we hold in balance incompatible and radically opposed views each of which seems exclusively true' (Rabkin 1977: 295). This has consequences when the accent is on meaning and effects on audiences: the starkest quality of the writing leading into a probable staging of the play is that these dualities are there to be solved in the more complex investigations of the work or papered over if one wants a quiet life. The yardstick for estimating the quality, therefore, of the reading or representation involves one in a search for where there are gestalt conundra and whether one dwells on them or avoids them.

Hamlet takes the opportunity to direct theatre, his choice *The Murder of Gonzago*. As a metatheatrical trope, it provides a pause as well as proof of Claudius's guilt. There is a distancing that allows analysis and a promotion of self-consciousness about theatrical illusion. The scene is one where we see illusion convey meanings directly to the audience as they also contribute to the plot.

In the confines of realism, we marvel at a facsimile accuracy, but that does not excise more lateral or paratactic allusions that work back on the plot; indeed, it should mean that it creates an expectation of thematic unity where cause and effect are clear and individual motivation seems just a trait of personality. In consideration of this view, this could be a means by which we might value the quality, for spectators, of a reassuring theatrical experience.

In our own contemporary frames of reference, we live in a deeply narrativized culture through more obviously fictional media – television, the simulations of online games, film, for example – that are easy to access and provide us with familiar genres and patternings of plot. The live qualities of any event in a theatre must now be measured against a predominance of experiences caused by recorded art. Philip Auslander's concept of 'liveness' captures that sense, even when we witness any live performance, of simulation, where witnessing bodies and words in 'real' time has undergone radical change: there is a blurring in our reception between 'live forms and mediatized ones', whose once separate ontologies have merged (Auslander 1999: 7). There are also crucial distinctions to be observed when mentioning *an* audience. Using Nicholas Abercrombie and Brian J. Longhurst's categories, there are significant paradigms of behaviour evident in simple, mass and diffused audiences (Abercrombie and Longhurst: 1998: 39–76). Shared with a sense of early modern theatre gatherings, there are still *simple* audiences for a live event in which spectators participate by gestures of approval or dissent. However, we now cannot dissociate ourselves from other connotations and experiences of participation in drama: the *mass* audience summoned by mass media and recorded performance that is scattered and yet privatized in response (and which is potentially congregated through reviews or chat rooms), and a *diffused* audience whose experiences are by no means common and, due to media saturation, is apt to regard performances as mundane.

The engagement with the playtext and its realization is thus caught between the complexities of ritual and spectacle. As Dennis Kennedy has reminded us, defining audiences (and thus a theory of response) is a complex matter – more so now than ever before. With an international scope, he investigates how Shakespeare and other Western cultural products achieve radically alternative meanings when subjected to the gaze (and separate needs) of audiences separated from an Anglo-American consensus, where recognized rituals permeate the year (Kennedy 2009: 204–6). In most forms of response to theatre or film, there is the invitation to render consumption as passive, or as rehearsed. Radical spectacle breaks up this patterning and thus reaches out to the spectator in unforeseen ways and so with less anticipated results (Kennedy 2009: 4–25).

Ophelia is puzzled at Hamlet's choice of play before the Danish court: 'What means this, my lord?', 'Belike this show imports the argument of the play', 'Will he tell us what the show meant?' (3.2.138, 141–2, 145). The attention of the here-and-now audience is rather less on the 'import' of the drama than how we see it affect Claudius, and possibly Gertrude. Is this a verification of the Ghost's message and so status? Will the performed action betray Gertrude too? The immediate locus of attention goes some way to resolving – for Hamlet – his own quandary. The play-within-a-play is a device, however, that possesses not just the status of imparting narrative information as it is linked by repetition to wider thematic issues.

The word 'show' itself is profoundly ambiguous across the play as a whole. Its spectrum of meaning spans just indicating in a neutral, demonstrative, sense and surface appearance (as in 'putting on a show'). It appears in both senses and it would register as an aural resonance in several key episodes. It is lent physical shape in the players' show before the court including the dumbshow, and Hamlet's 'antic disposition' that he fleshes out with what he takes to be customary traits (1.5.178–88) that verge on (stage) clownish display. In a macro sense, there is much that can derive from this ambiguity: how can we be sure that what is shown is authentic in the most empirical sense? Can we trust in our own notion of consistent selfhood, amounting to our 'character'? As early as our first meeting with Hamlet, he is playing a part, according to Gertrude, who requires that he 'cast [his] nightly colour off', yet Hamlet 'knows not "seems"', or the 'shapes of grief', for he has 'that within which passeth show' (1.2.68, 76, 82, 85). It is not the first time that we have heard these references to keeping up appearances, as we might register an echo of Marcellus's irony that 'the show of violence' before the Ghost is really an act of 'malicious mockery', given its immaterial being (1.1.149,150) – or Cornelius's and Voltemand's 'show' of duty to the king (1.2.40), or Laertes' return from France to 'show [his] duty' by attending the coronation (1.2.53). The question emerges thereby as to how one might ascertain true worth or the accuracy of deictic gestures. Why does one need so many gestures of this order in Elsinore?

There is a journey taken by Hamlet en route to his corpse brought by 'four captains ... to the stage' (5.2.402–3), a spectacle wherein 'soldier's music and the rites of war' (5.2.406–7) would 'speak loudly for him' (5.2.406). Hamlet's end is only partially appropriate, for the homophone 'rites/ rights' is susceptible to at least two distinct readings, both possible: he is to be interred fittingly in a fashion to be expected at a time of conflict, and/or he is a prize for the victor. Fortinbras himself in the last scene finds that the charnel house appearance of so many bodies is a spectacle that 'shows much amiss' (5.2.409). Both semes might leave a spectator wondering about the military context accorded him, the 'show' that does not tally with what we have witnessed about the student prince throughout the narrative.

Against this backdrop, we would note that there is a distinct aural power in repetition, and the frequency that can be noted about how the less neutral significations of 'show' echo in certain portions of the narrative would carry its own power. Not all narrative threads derive from linear spacing and an appreciation of consequences derived from deliberative human action. Thus, Ophelia is instructed by Polonius not to take on trust Hamlet's vows much as they resemble 'brokers' who may behave like 'sanctified and pious bawds' who 'show' [impress] by display their 'investments' (1.3.127–30). However, Polonius is infected by this disjuncture between appearance and inner worth. Hiding behind the arras, he and Claudius in their own way try to discover a truth about Hamlet's behaviour. The staged quality of this episode is clear. Polonius orders Ophelia to walk with a book, 'that show of such an exercise may colour / Your loneliness' (3.1.45–6). The next time we see Polonius hiding behind an arras is when he is stabbed through its fabric by Hamlet – in a perhaps thrilling attempt to strike out through falsehood and disguise. Polonius sets this up as a ruse by which Hamlet might 'show his griefs' to Gertrude (3.1.184).

These aspects of representation pose questions that have their apogee in the play designed to catch Claudius's conscience. Perhaps plays in general are designed to do just that, and Hamlet's relationship with the players is one of kinship. At his first sight of them, he seems to struggle with how to host them genuinely: 'The appurtenance of welcome is fashion and ceremony. Let me comply with you in this garb – lest my extent to the players, which I tell you, must show fairly outwards, should more appear like entertainment than yours' (2.2.372–6). There seems infinite recession here: actors are well versed in plausible show, yet the occasion of welcome demands a convergence of show and authenticity of sentiment in that some acceptable 'show' of hospitality is conventionally necessary. Much like Cordelia, when required to heave daughterly love into words for Lear, she finds words get in the way, and 'nothing' is the appropriate response (1.1.87). Drama requires words and its tools are outward gesture and show.

There is a continuity in Hamlet's advice to the players that reaches out to any audience. Town criers – no matter how loud their address to us – do not quite convince by simple volume, nor is it convincing to 'saw the air too much' (3.2.4) to suggest passion. Instead, Hamlet advises a 'smoothness' in delivery, part of a 'temperance' that dispenses with oratorical rhetoric (and not quite in line with the conventional polish of both the Dido/Aeneas/Priam's daughter epic histrionics (2.2.451–519) and also the murder of Gonzago that has such a radical effect on its on-stage audience). There is contradiction here, however, as the formally poetic lines that the Player King utters and the dumbshow are seen to have an immediate effect in unearthing Claudius's guilt, whereas, by extension, the less formally poetic speeches of much of the other stage action, it is hoped, will have a similar effect on the auditorium audience.

Returning to the sense of a public sphere, there is manifested a subtle but still noticeable shift in the self-consciousness of a Globe or Blackfriars gathering. In granting evaluative access to the plotting of the play, Shakespeare co-opts a varied auditory in tracing the trappings of authority and an opportunity to see beyond them – but to what? Hamlet might indeed assert that he has that within that passes show, and, if we are convinced, then we are granting an interior intuition a superiority over any status rights. It is also an ingredient in a reflex of Calvinist theology and devotional ethics. As James Simpson describes in relation to the emergence of a Protestant aesthetics during Shakespeare's writing career, even if there were theatres within the 'Liberties', it was also a time of extreme and gathering government interest in the consequences of secular art, extending to regulation on a scale that was sudden and potentially interventionist. The targets of this surveillance are perhaps surprising: portrayal of the sacraments would be likely to provoke the ire of Commissioners, and this – at the same time as the opening of so many public theatres – led to a piecemeal suppression of cycle plays. Staging overt devotional drama was a risk. Secular fictions were less so (Simpson 2019: 201–34). The 1559 ban of religion appearing in plays simply meant that the deeper recesses of belief could not be portrayed as a significant contribution to any collective identity. Instead, dramatists appealed to political alignments, usually as regards the nation, to achieve a sense of community.

It is the pivotal role of theatre that Shakespeare and his contemporaries exploited; on the one hand, it operated as a means to produce a fresh and very relevant art form, one that illustrated the dualities of humanism, of choice and personal responsibility, yet on the other hand, it also portrayed a struggle to break free of the fears of Calvinism as an alternative to residual Catholicism. Along the way, one threaded a path towards a 'truth' freed of an implicit belief in the ritualistic and cyclic, and the shows of the world. As Grace Tiffany has shown, there was a vein of deep scepticism about the 'shows' of theatre – and oratory and not just in anti-theatrical views (Tiffany 2003). Anthony Munday felt that there was guilt foisted upon 'actors and beholders alike' when they gave themselves up to be witnesses of impersonation or 'low' material: 'So that in that representation of whoredom, all the people in mind play the whores' (Munday 1590: 3).

Remembering Ecclesiasticus 13.1, one could conclude that 'he that toucheth pitch shall be defiled therewith; and he that hath fellowship with a proud man shall be like unto him' (King James Version).

The seventeenth of the thirty-nine articles, 'Of Predestination and Election', is worth quoting at length:

> Predestination to Life is the everlasting purpose of God, whereby (before the foundations of the world were laid) he hath constantly decreed by his counsel secret to us, to deliver from curse and damnation those whom he hath chosen in Christ out of mankind, and to bring them by Christ to everlasting salvation, as vessels made to honour. Wherefore, they which be endued with so excellent a benefit of God be called according to God's purpose by his Spirit working in due season: they through Grace obey the calling: they be justified freely: they be made sons of God by adoption: they be made like the image of his only-begotten Son Jesus Christ: they walk religiously in good works, and at length, by God's mercy, they attain to everlasting felicity.

But only the elect have a happy ending, and this is according to a 'counsel secret to us', whereby the award of grace is beyond our powers of prediction or action to intervene.[11] If one peers closely at the deeper effects of this form of Calvinism, then we might construct an early modern audience that is already on a cosmic stage, where God is the spectator (see Cannon 1971; Katz 2018; Kaufman 2006). Correspondingly, the boundaries of public and private dissolve.

Our own sense of the private is much more conditioned by physical boundaries than most of Shakespeare's spectators. In many ways, our culture has given us a sense of choice and an illusion of self-determination; our living space is better defined and we can choose to have our culture individually and apart much more than the regular Jaques or Timon figure. We are used to being a biddable audience and politeness reigns in most (but not all) social gatherings. At a time of so much electronic scrutiny and immediate access (whether desired or not), however, we cannot always have the luxury of evading surveillance. We might listen to the traces that Shakespeare's audiences have left behind and wonder whether we have not lost something in the entry to technical mastery.

Conclusion

As I write in 2020, the world is deprived of live performance before known and visible spectators thanks to a pandemic that – as we now contemplate the future – is likely to have far-reaching consequences for theatre and its economic basis. There is some hope that smaller-scale and unorthodox forms of Shakespeare will still thrive during this period, and that the desire for the poetry and live comment of his plays can still be celebrated, even if only through memory. We have not been here before in quite this way, although there are some equivalent moments to contemplate: the advent of film that was widely predicted as an overpowering competitor to theatre in the mid-twentieth century, and the closing of the theatres due to plague in early modern London that, even if to some extent a political expedient, still deeply affected Shakespeare himself. What is now known as bubonic plague was first evident in December 1592, and it led to a closure of the public theatres in 1593, 1603 and 1608. Shakespeare's son, Hamnet, died of the infection in 1596, when he was just eleven. For the time being, we are heavily dependent on technology to allow us a measure of witness to Shakespeare.

Performance has always been capable, however, of capitalizing on technological advances, or – if one were so minded – to ignore them intentionally to signify a sense of past purity with a bare stage and/or to return to what could be taken as 'original' Shakespeare. The world of the poor itinerant player, Lear's fool, the nomadic Feste from *Twelfth Night* or *As You Like It*'s Jaques, for example, are appealing as they gesture towards some zero degree of truth telling. In recent times, Jerzy Grotowski's plea for a 'poor theatre' was motivated by the need for an intimate communion between actor and spectator, an act of 'integration, the discarding of masks, the revealing of the real substance: a totality of physical and mental reactions' (Grotowski with Flaszen 1968: 255). What at the outset might appear upsetting or at least unsettling is apt in time and by imitation to dwindle into the expected and conventional. The shock of the new might evade the customary, but not for all time. Hence, it is that Peter Brook embraced the thrill of the empty space, where theatre is created simply by allowing a man to walk across such a space while another observes him (Brook 1968: 9). After regular contact, say, with Beckett, one might require more from a modern theatre, a moving on from the existentialist moment. This hope that the word painting of Shakespearean language was scenery enough was captured most influentially enough in J. L. Styan's *The Shakespeare Revolution: Criticism and Performance in the Twentieth Century* (Styan 1977), whose survey of Shakespearean reception maps the contribution of practitioners alongside textual editors and theatre historians – indeed, gives them precedence in some quarters.

Some forms of technology may seem to promote the means and not the end result, an enhanced intimacy with a spectator or a provocation that produces an active imagination. The digital world we now have to inhabit produces questions that reach out to the very bases of cognition and motivation. We are geared up to assimilate the new and challenging and therefore render it familiar in order to comprehend it. This has consequences for any radical performance in that, while it refuses to rely on the well-trodden paths of meaning and significance, it also has to establish for the spectator new directions to replace them. In Pascale Aebischer's investigation of how the technological affects spectatorship, she notes how the scenic context for any spoken word is foregrounded in the forms of theatrical communication, such as the placing of an audience, the refusal of lighting to demarcate securely a distance between the stage and auditorium, the verbal magic replaced by various methods of manifestation. Her conclusion is less a definitive summation than a staging-post, anticipating further conversations about the ethics of this shock of the new. The ways in which audiences might become 'co-producers of plotlines that were only implicit in the plays' and aware of the 'often invisible structures that underpin the plays' are enhanced by the methods by which we are caught 'off guard' by technology or wherein we encounter the texts in ways we could not have done before (Aebischer 2017: 318).[1] What W. B. Worthen terms 'technicity' (Worthen 2017: 321–40), however, has always accompanied any theatrical representation; once the Globe must have appeared technically resourceful.

These two poles of the viewing spectrum – bare stage to technically enhanced spectacle – are choices both wedded to creating the alert spectator: one by reduction, the other by shock tactics. The methods are strategically various and new digital resources – perhaps by means of their untried and unrehearsed effects – have the advantage of a radical contract with the intended audience. Stephen Purcell's attempt to capture the ways that audiences for Shakespeare are constructed hits an impasse, a hermeneutic circle where audiences feel free (they have paid to see the company perform . . .) yet they also surrender some of that freedom with the entrance fee. His list of politely (or not so courteously) coercive means is a various one, where audiences 'play at being audiences, whether self-consciously or not, by the very fact that they adopt certain behaviours as a group and in response to that group' (Purcell 2013: 150; Findlay 2018). We now must consider effects upon a dispersed audience.

The issues associated with what we might now do with Shakespeare are multiple – and multiplying. He is beyond a bare celebration in that he is (alas!) a national treasure, leading to the conclusion that we think we *know* his work through allusion and turns of phrase (note the titles of thriller or detective novels, for example). In terms of identifying his aesthetic effect or estimating how we might escape the coercion of our 'interpretive community', though, the great virtue of his craft is that we are part of its effect if we focus on the emotive and instinctual aspects of what is produced out of the text and where we might meet the power of the unexpected and even uncomfortable. Residing in our comfort zones, we often admire craft and the satisfaction of rituals confirmed at arm's length so as to keep ourselves uncontaminated by shock or the troubling incursion of truly radical experiences. This search for what we did not anticipate knowing about any Shakespeare text must involve us in a level of divorce from our own inherited history and cultural preconception, a process of 'unlearning' leading to an openness to the endeavour of responsiveness. There is evidence that Shakespeare's first audiences had already ventured onto this terrain simply en route to the Bankside auditoria or to the second Blackfriars theatre, recently converted from a Dominican priory just over the Thames. Geographically, it was a Fringe event – and psychologically too, in its appeal to popular memory.

To a degree, it has always been thus. Sir Philip Sidney mused on the role of the theatre in his neo-platonic *An Apology for Poetry* (written 1579–80; published posthumously, 1595) and wrestled with its imitative display. On the one hand, no poet may 'make circles about your imagination, to conjure you to believe for true what he writes'. On the other, there is a validity about such art in the same way that no child attending a play and seeing '*Thebes* written in great letters upon an old door' will mistake it for a reality (Sidney 2002: 103). The crucial distinction, Sidney notes, lies in a difference between reporting (the province of the historian) and representing, where aspirations or glimpses of the ideal can be figured. What Sidney recognizes (in terms that resemble our own distinction between showing and telling) is that any departure from strict 'reporting' does not erode art's capacity to relay truth. On the other hand, that latitude could bring in mixed modes of response, not just problematic hybrids such as tragi-comedies, but also that satiric levelling so distrusted by anti-theatrical commentators, where one might 'thrust in clowns by head and shoulders, to play a part in majestical matters, with neither decency and commiseration' (Sidney 2002: 111–12). While opening the door to non-literal truth, Sidney is at pains to demonstrate the dangers of a free-for-all, where the class system is questioned.

The path towards assessing our own 'public sphere' wherein we consume Shakespeare encounters the need to assess similar questions, and, if we depart from the keen observation and imitative skill of our own mimetic needs, what results? Where might we find common ground in our subjectivity with others (see Wood 2018)? There has always been this unanalytical element about response studies, yet that does not prevent the search for common phenomenological terms. Where Shakespeare is concerned, the myth precedes any theatrical experience and the reluctance to interpret and adapt derives from our more nostalgic impulses, to retreat and escape in some costume drama of the mind. Yet this community of interest can take too many anaesthetic shortcuts: how can we differentiate this drive to typification and consumerist comfort from the daring of awkwardness and a heterodox faith in one's own individuality?

In 1934, John Dewey posed the question as to what 'having an experience' might be, and he found it interesting to investigate but, by definition, always out of analytic reach. It should be so, for unless there is a perceivable link between the aesthetic representation of 'the world' and our inner world, then we recognize but do not own the experience. We observe but hold any creation at arm's length, yet, in so doing, we no longer possess it. As far as the stage is concerned, the physical demarcation of stage space and our secure seat in the stalls has to be overcome psychologically and even spiritually if Dewey's prescription for an experience has any resonance (Dewey 1934: 36–59). We have to consider the possibility of surrender.

The first consideration is that inherited conceptions might pre-empt sensation, and history might provide the categories for meaning that appear exhaustive. As a basic condition of cognition, how we gain knowledge, the mind is never blank; when new experiences are caused, their strength and significance is not registered on account of qualities immanent in the nominal source. Kings in drama are not always typically regal, a tragic flaw might be vast (even if ultimately excusable), and so we can shield ourselves from registering it as a weakness we might easily possess, or the tragedy might lie in our stars, not deep within us. What is Rome in *Julius Caesar* or *Antony and Cleopatra*, or Athens in *A Midsummer Night's Dream* or *Timon of Athens*? Furthermore, does any playtext establish a range of audience reactions during performance? We live in a more obviously narrativized culture than in the early modern era thanks to the currency of soap operas and film, and Shakespeare's legacy can tend to be an arena of ideological struggle. 'He' can be taken to uphold tradition and Englishness, a timeless continuity of values and therefore of the status quo, but this, when viewed ideologically, is a cue for nostalgia. John Frow prefers to see a fixation with the 'safe' past as a cultural pat on one's own back, a cultural capital that 'is meant to place the discussion on the level of aesthetic competencies rather than on the level of social class'. There would appear to be a matter of more meaningful complexity and craft, yet he is distrustful of the 'aesthetic' because it 'is immediately a code word for class' (Frow 1991: 148). How directly, therefore, does a Shakespeare play speak to us?

Once we release ourselves from 'Shakespeare' in matters of measuring how his dramatic strategies operate upon us *now*, we find a creativity that should be more responsive to theatrical experiment. The logical extension of this realization is that what ultimately counts is a 'present' in which instinctive feelings contribute to meaning. 'Presentism' prioritizes an isolation of the contemporary as a distinct zone apart from how memory or fears/hopes operate upon the present. This demands complex distinctions.[2] Its project, however, does derive from a desire to liberate response. For Walter Benjamin, in his 'Theses on the Philosophy of History', the past 'is the subject of a structure whose site is not homogenous, empty time, but time filled by the presence of the now' (Benjamin 1968: 261), and it is essential to note that the full context of 'the now' – as summed up by Harry Zohn (his translator) – is that the original *Jetztzeit* does not indicate any static ontology (whereby we rely on a rather daunting attempt to sum up all that could be felt or recognized in the snapshot of the present) but rather a consciousness of the 'now', wherein, to adopt Evelyn Gajowski's synopsis: 'we cannot help but be influenced in our apprehension of Shakespeare's texts by contemporary discursive practices, ideologies, and events that constitute us, even as we, in turn, constitute Shakespeare's texts' (Gajowski 2009: 6). This entails a privileging of 'present' needs, politically and culturally, over past practices (even if we inevitably build upon an inherited knowledge).[3]

What is laudable in theory affects practice in subtly alternative ways and the relative freedoms suggested by such a focus open up related questions of relevance and utility. In George Lakoff and Mark Johnson's analysis of metaphors as conceptual structures, a pure freedom of thought is exceptional, if not impossible, in that the very basis of thought processes lies in the figurative, either as a starting point or, at least, as the necessary anchor for a development of cognition. In other words, metaphors are not exclusively a matter of language; we are not fooled by a sign over a door claiming that this scene is set in Thebes, but that suspension of belief is easily supplanted by a parade of collateral questions: what might Thebes bring to mind that any equivalent location from southern Europe could not? Caliban's deformity means what: a site of pity or revulsion? Are kings (or any authority figures) innately of a superior status, or are they necessary, pragmatically speaking, as just a lynchpin of order, where through the ceremony of obedience and *droit de seigneur* they are where they are? Inevitably, dramatic locations and characters are divested of any absolute existence because they are at root signs, not free-standing entities. We are constantly invited to subscribe to, as they put it, the 'Myth of Objectivism', yet our world is governed by a more relational consciousness, where our sense of the 'real' requires

- viewing objects only as entities relative to our interactions with the world and our projections on it:
- viewing properties as interactional rather than inherent;
- viewing categories as experiential gestalts defined via prototype instead of viewing them as rigidly fixed and defined via set theory. (Lakoff and Johnson 2003: 210)

We ground metaphors in the particular where whatever might be intended as a signified content cannot be kept separate from the vehicle that expresses it. Whenever there may be 'dynamic brain functions', where there is an effort at interpreting complex and recondite signs or actions, there is a process of *'enactment'* (Lakoff and Johnson 1980: 257). This is not a purely intellectual exercise as the punctuation marks and stresses in this activity are neural, involving the visual and motor cortices. We may be guided at the first by some sense of communal recognition – it would be a basic and traditional assumption that associations of Britishness would be misplaced if applied to New York, or that murder is a regular (and so natural) human instinct – but that does not take us very far. That is because any initial metaphor does not stay still in drama, but gives rise to 'inference patterns' that cannot be sustained or governed solely by where they started because the action of the enactment (for the actor and the spectator) combines basic figures to pursue more complex formations; the duration of the narrative cannot help but introduce additions that extend the abstract or conventional in an application to events and character development (Lakoff and Johnson 1980: 252–61).[4]

In its terms of reference, this theoretical perception spreads out into wider psychological frames. In Daniel Kahneman's *Thinking, Fast and Slow* (2011), he contrasts two modes of thinking, loosely defined as alternative systems of cognition. The first is instinctive and 'fast' in that it lies largely outside of our control and where we react to visual stimuli on a threat/

pleasure axis. If we see a film of a train or fierce animal coming swiftly towards us, the range of possible reactions is limited, as we cannot often control them. The second is more deliberative as with solving mathematical problems, where attention has to be paid to matters of 'agency, choice, and concentration' in order to be successful (Kahneman 2011: 21). We are aided in this task by certain inherited conventions so that we are better placed to get to an accurate answer.

The disquieting reflection Kahneman leads us towards is that there are few such deliberative mental operations that are completely free of that 'fast' ingredient supposedly quite distinct in kind and effect. We might come away from a night at the theatre with an immediate and probably value-laden reaction. We might have taken a dislike to the whole performance or perhaps to certain episodes and that is that. When forced to think more deeply about those judgements, it is likely that we have to interrogate our motives for approval or not and root out the adventitious from the fundamental. We may be confronted by other views in a seminar or just a conversation in a bar or pub immediately afterwards that conflict with or supplement our own. Gradually, we move away from the originating performance to an adjacent sphere of debate, where we are encouraged to negotiate with others or fall back on our own reactions. This is analogous to how response theories operate, for that immediate reaction need not be cancelled out completely by an apparently more judicious one, but it can be extended and understood better. Indeed, the path to identifying what is authentically individual about our evaluations and how we respond is to isolate how we are encouraged to be analytical or 'safe' in our aesthetic perspectives and part them from that 'fast' impulse.

Whilst Kahneman's examples are drawn mainly from accounts of economic risk taking and the predictive models that accompany them, he opens out his investigations into wider areas of debate that bear upon all aspects of judgement and comprehension. There are two further reflections of his that we might bear in mind when looking closely at the various response approaches to Shakespeare. In order to reveal how we might treat dramatic texts as special cases of communication, we might question whether a consistent deployment of first principles (in theory) accomplishes just what studies of response seek to uncover. Kahneman's phrase for this wariness is 'theory-induced blindness', where any acceptance of a particular conceptual perspective brings in its wake an inability to trace its flaws: 'If you come across an observation that does not seem to fit the model, you assume that there must be a perfectly good explanation that you are somehow missing ' (Kahneman 2011: 277). This does not mean that one should simply treat response theorists as given to randomness and impressionism; it is just that certain priorities in the process of interpretation and analyses of aesthetic experience encounter exceptions to rules as such. For Kahneman, any clear view of 'rare events' in an economy is usually discounted on a percentage basis so that any prediction might be more forceful and contribute to policy. Conversely, we might be mindful of items that are so arresting and of memorable interest that we 'overweight' them in significance even if we realize that they cannot be a contribution to global tendencies (Kahneman 2011: 322–3). Once we accept that literary expression is significantly distinct from normal or 'real-world' verbal exchanges, then linguistic conventions help us only up to a point. We also might distrust the conventions that emerge from poetics and, as far as drama is concerned, any consensus as to the best plays. An identification of how we judge and respond, however, is no luxury. What might be a 'rare event', truly original in its effects, might disturb us yet in the service of psychological benefit and an expansion of our perceptual horizons. In short, it is of value to dwell on what constitutes an arresting and radical experience and to find the means to explain it.

In conclusion, it could be said that response theories contribute to assessing Shakespeare as performed in at least four areas:

1 they enable us to register as a vital component the instinctual witness of performance;
2 they permit us to consider the place of creativity when registering any staged meaning, and thus an emancipation of us as spectators and, one hopes, performers;
3 they bring to consciousness non-traditional educational methods the aims of which are to *realize* Shakespeare and to grant these approaches a relevance alongside other theoretical investigations; and
4 they enlarge our entry into any spectrum of taste and aesthetic evaluation by focusing on how the individual could prise the self away from tradition and any normative senses of how drama may be 'consumed'.

These encounters with Shakespeare radiate out into wider analyses that quiz our comprehension of the very process of acting and observing outside the theatre, bringing into play a 'pensiveness', as Rancière understands the term, that alerts us to possibilities that otherwise elude us in everyday social negotiation. Finally, it allows us to contemplate what survives, even if these norms are under attack or are undergoing radical change.

APPENDIX

Podcast interviews with the authors of many of the titles in the *Arden Shakespeare and Theory* series are available. Details of both published and forthcoming titles are listed below.

Shakespeare and Cultural Materialist Theory, Christopher Marlow http://blogs.surrey.ac.uk/shakespeare/2016/11/04/shakespeare-and-contemporary-theory-31-shakespeare-and-cultural-materialist-theory-with-christopher-marlow/

Shakespeare and Ecocritical Theory, Gabriel Egan http://blogs.surrey.ac.uk/shakespeare/2016/05/20/shakespeare-and-contemporary-theory-24-shakespeare-and-ecocritical-theory-with-gabriel-egan/

Shakespeare and Ecofeminist Theory, Rebecca Laroche and Jennifer Munroe http://blogs.surrey.ac.uk/shakespeare/2016/06/07/shakespeare-and-contemporary-theory-25-shakespeare-and-ecofeminist-theory-with-rebecca-laroche-and-jennifer-munroe/

Shakespeare and Economic Theory, David Hawkes http://blogs.surrey.ac.uk/shakespeare/2016/05/05/shakespeare-and-contemporary-theory-22-shakespeare-and-economic-theory-with-david-hawkes/

Shakespeare and Feminist Theory, Marianne Novy http://blogs.surrey.ac.uk/shakespeare/2016/05/13/shakespeare-and-contemporary-theory-23-shakespeare-and-feminist-theory-with-marianne-novy/

Shakespeare and New Historicist Theory, Neema Parvini http://blogs.surrey.ac.uk/shakespeare/2016/08/29/

shakespeare-and-contemporary-theory-27-shakespeare-and-new-historicist-theory-with-evelyn-gajowski-and-neema-parvini/

Shakespeare and Postcolonial Theory, Jyotsna G. Singh http://blogs.surrey.ac.uk/shakespeare/2016/07/19/shakespeare-and-contemporary-theory-26-shakespeare-and-postcolonial-theory-with-jyotsna-singh/

Shakespeare and Posthumanist Theory, Karen Raber http://blogs.surrey.ac.uk/shakespeare/2016/09/30/shakespeare-and-contemporary-theory-28-shakespeare-and-posthumanist-theory-with-karen-raber/

Shakespeare and Presentist Theory, Evelyn Gajowski http://blogs.surrey.ac.uk/shakespeare/2016/04/29/shakespeare-and-contemporary-theory-21-the-arden-shakespeare-and-theory-series-with-evelyn-gajowski/

Shakespeare and Queer Theory, Melissa E. Sanchez http://blogs.surrey.ac.uk/shakespeare/2016/10/18/shakespeare-and-contemporary-theory-29-shakespeare-and-queer-theory-with-melissa-e-sanchez/

NOTES

Introduction

1 Unless otherwise indicated, the Shakespeare texts adopted for this study are from *The Arden Shakespeare Complete Works*, ed. Ann Thompson, David Scott Kastan and Richard Proudfoot (2011).

Chapter 1

1 The most succinct summaries can be found in Bell 1990: 161–7 and Zahavi 2015: 177–94.
2 See the definition in Husserl 1982: 242–3. The process of how this leads to evaluation is summed up in one of Husserl's late works from 1939 (Husserl 1973).
3 This is more comprehensively explained in two essays in Gadamer 2019: 'Historicity and Truth' (1991: 13–23) and 'The History of the Universe and the Historicity of Human Beings' (1988: 25–41).
4 The explanation of drama's borderline elements is contained at Ingarden: 1973a: 317–23.
5 A fuller context for this verdict can be found in Sartre's discussion with those attending in Rome in 'Art and Subjectivity' (Sartre 2016: 68–110).
6 This is the basis for Georges Poulet's apology for critical assessment, in that the motivated response provided by the deepest readings allows the 'object' before us (book, script or performance) to disappear. Consequently, we are affected in the process: 'Reading . . . is the act in which the subjective principle which I call *I*, is modified in such a way that I no longer have the

right, strictly speaking, to consider it as my *I*. I am on loan to another' (Poulet 1980: 45).

7   See Brown's succinct summary of Freud's contribution to Shakespeare studies (2015: 11–21).

8   See Cook's valuable survey of embodied performance in her whole essay (2013: 83–90) and Neal Utterback's revisioning of the role that memory plays in delving into body and self-projection that forms the basis of building a role for performance (Utterback 2013: 147–58). His cognitive experiments underpin the view that our conscious selves achieve meanings through creative recall: 'Who we are as conscious selves is a story we tell ourselves' (Utterback 2013: 153).

9   Drawing on Jean Mandler's work on 'image schemas' (Mandler 1984), Mary Thomas Crane applies the interrelatedness of such sensory networks with Shakespeare's linguistic features to suggest a distinctiveness in his metaphorical landscape (Crane 2001: especially 1–35).

10 See his application of this term in McConachie 2008: 65–120 (especially 73–7). The term 'affordances' was originally James J Gibson's in Gibson 1979 where he examined the disposition of objects around and between which actors move and create character.

11 See also his essay 'Introduction: Spectating as Sandbox Play', in McConachie 2013: 183–98.

Chapter 2

1   The most incisive account is W. B.Worthen's (1986). A valuable updating can be found in Richard Madelaine's 'Shakespeare in Production' edition of the play (Madelaine 1998: especially 288–94). Pointing towards the motivation for the scene's ironies, Martha Tuck Rozett fails to take account of the complexities of audience response (Rozett 1985); the conclusion that there is something 'timeless' in 'the paradoxical way in which lovers alternately torment and celebrate one another' (Rozett 1985: 164) perhaps needs supplementing by accounts of how the hybridity of the tragedy has attracted responses that are neither predictable nor perennial.

2 The dramatic equivalence of this could be derived from Plutarch, where Charmian is found at this point 'trimming the Diademe which [she] ware upon her head' (Bullough 1957–75: 5: 316).

3 One could also claim that the gender issues could be obscured in an all-male cast such as at the Globe in 1999, when Mark Rylance played the Queen.

4 For example, Charles Spencer, *Telegraph*, 14 November 2013: while Antony is very tall, 'in contrast his American Cleopatra, Joaquina Kalukango, is very short. It's the little and large show, and more comic than sexy.'

5 See also Hamer 1996: 'It is by taking the part of Cleopatra, speaking out of the predicament he finds her to be in, that Shakespeare will find, if at all, a way that is not the Roman one to understand her story' (75).

6 See also Iser 1981. Fish's protracted objections to Iser's division between a tangible real environment and one that arises out of an imaginative involvement occurs in the next issue of *Diacritics*.

7 For more on this kind of support, see Fluck 2000; Armstrong 2000 and Thomas 2008.

Chapter 3

1 A useful conspectus of Renaissance concepts of the dream can be found in Mandel 1973, and the overlap between the imaginative and the investigative in the early modern era is the main thesis of Cowan 2016.

2 The term is taken from the third essay ('Archetypal Criticism') in Frye 1957: 182–4, where he traces – especially in Shakespeare's comedies – a movement away from a recognizable world, where the motive is to imitate normality, to a 'green' alternative where the straitjackets of acceptability are removed and repressed desire released before a reversion to the original world where there is the possibility that 'winter' has been defeated and fertility victorious. There is also the tendency, however, for 'normality' no longer to appear quite so as a consequence of the return.

3 Oberon's possible cruelty is emphasized by the repetition of the danger in this trick when he wishes to restore her from 'the hateful imperfection of her eyes' once he has regained the Indian boy (4.1.62).

4 The fullest account of his varied status can be found in Peter Holland (1994: 35–49). On the one hand, he is the 'merry wanderer of the night' (2.1.43) and the drudge who indulges in practical jokes; on the other, he is an image of the devil, given to confound normality.

5 The potential for darker nuances in the play is explored in Hutton 1985 and Hugh Grady makes the point that, while the action of the play seems fixed upon aesthetic diversion, once we examine the detail, we might discern its concerns with the limits of art (Grady 2008).

6 This is succinctly defined in Holland 1980.

7 Kuhn's *The Structure of Scientific Revolutions* (Kuhn 1962) posits the idea that scientific discoveries arise due to timing, both due to the perceived need for certain problems to be solved and a need for order that fluctuates according to temporal context.

8 Bleich notes this impasse and turns it into a positive Bleich (1978: 87–93). The Freud text is from his 'The *Moses* of Michelangelo' (1914), in Rieff 1963: 81.

9 By 1981, Culler conceded that any concept of an ideal or super-reader (who possessed compendious contextual and hermeneutic knowledge) was beside the point, as one's attention might be more drawn to a divergence of readings (and why they coexist) than any superior master interpretation. Readings are not open to infinite improvement as they also have a historically located relevance. At any one time, 'competence' signifies being conversant with a culture's accepted norms without which interpretation would be incomprehensible (see Culler 1981: 50–9).

10 The fullest summary of these levels of intelligibility are to be found in Culler 1975: 139–45.

11 See Freund 1987: 129–30; Ray 1984: 87–9, and Jane Tompkins's review of Bleich's *Subjective Criticism* (Tompkins 1978).

12 For a fuller discussion of Fish's ideas of interpretive change, see Dasenbrock 1986 and Stecker 1990.

13 See also Graff 1985.

Chapter 4

1 For a careful analysis of the resistant elements in Wesker's work, see Sicher 1991.
2 See Metzger 1998; Hirschfeld 2006; Shapiro 1996: 157–65.
3 We are reminded of this cogently by D. M. Cohen: 'If it is true that Jewishness in the play is equated with wickedness, it is surely unlikely that Shylock's elaborate rationalizations of his behaviour are intended to render him as sympathetic' (Cohen 1980: 60).
4 This issue derived from naming and innate identity also surrounds the stage directions that describe his death and removal from the stage at 5.6.130 and *s.d.,* 154, where he reappears as 'Martius'.
5 This is clear in the contemporary extracts included in Geoffrey Bullough's section on the play in Bullough 1957–75: V: 509, 553–63.
6 See 1.9.7 (Cominius on the 'fusty plebeians); 2.1.9, and 2.1.94–5, where it could be said Menenius shows his true colours in now casting the plebeians as 'hungry' in desiring to 'devour' Martius, and 'beastly' in that any 'conversation' with their tribunes would 'infect [his] brain'; 2.1.93–4, where Coriolanus has it that the patricians would become plebeians in bowing to their opinion ('You are plebeians / If they be senators' (3.1.101–2)) and 3.3, where the fickleness of the plebeians seems mob-like in their treatment of Brutus.
7 Lee Bliss's commentary at this point in her Cambridge edition correctly interprets this incursion as the appearance of a 'disorderly mob', whereby Shakespeare appears to see them as an 'undifferentiated political faction manipulated by the tribunes, not the reasonable individuals of earlier scenes' (Bliss 2000: 189). For further comment, see Wood 2011 and Shrank 2003.
8 This could be deduced as early as Menenius's Fable of the Belly that, as the action progresses, is more probably political expediency than a reliable reflection upon how matters stood. See Riss 1992.
9 See Parker 1994: 37–43; Kuzner 2007.

10 See Barbara Hodgdon's survey of this collision between alternative narratives in her edition of the play (Hodgdon 2010: 35–71).

11 For Emily Detmer, this taming could have been regarded – at the time – as a humane development, stopping short of wife-beating and other forms of silencing (Detmer 1997).

12 The textual situation of *A Shrew* is discussed at length by Hodgdon (2010: 23–8, 395–8); the most comprehensive account of how the similarity between the two plays might have an impact on interpretation is provided by Richard Hosley (1961, 1964).

13 Coleridge's 'table' is a reference to his admission that there are phenomena external to our consciousness found in his *Biographia Literaria* (1817): 'It is the table itself, which the man of common sense believes himself to see, not the phantom of a table, from which he may argumentatively deduce the reality of a table, which he does not see. If to destroy the reality of all, that we actually behold, be idealism, what can be more egregiously so, than the system of modern metaphysics, which banishes us to a land of shadows, surrounds us with apparitions, and distinguishes truth from illusion only by the majority of those who dream the same dream ?' The errant philosophers 'despise the faith [in the real] as the prejudice of the ignorant vulgar, because they live and move in a crowd of phrases and notions from which human nature has long ago vanished' (Coleridge 1983: 261–2, 263).

14 Hirsch – while not forsaking his earlier boldness – does qualify his bases for rejecting anachronistic approaches: see Hirsch 1983, 1984.

15 This aspect is enlarged upon by Felperin 1995, Brown 1985 and Greenblatt 1988: 129–63.

16 See Kennedy 2009: 115–32 (especially 120–5), Brotton 1998 and Loomba 1996.

17 The question as to whether we are encouraged to look beyond the aural and visual display is key to contriving a means to resist the play's more traditional interpreters. See Smith, B. 1999: 335–9 and, in more general terms, Smith, S. 2017: 130–6.

18 This argument is more expansively explained in Dimock 1991.

Chapter 5

1 See his retention of the yardstick of reason in his essay, 'Theory of Rationality and Theory of Meaning', in Habermas 2018.
2 See Stern 2009, Steggle 2020 and (with wider historical range) Balme 2014.
3 See Bruster 2000 and Clegg 2017, especially 120–79 (on *Richard II*).
4 This distrust of public theatre response is described at length by John Gordon Sweeney III, in Sweeney 1985: 3–16, 47–69 (where the Blackfriars audience is specifically the focus for *Sejanus*).
5 See Specter 2010: 133–70, Müller-Doohm 2016: 276–304.
6 This identification of its first 'placement' derives from Stern 2004: 15.
7 For more on this transition and its probable impact on audiences (and thus on altered methods of staging), see Mullaney 1988: 26–59; Gurr 1996: 169–75; Gurr 2009: 190–6; Dillon 2000: 20–42; Dustagheer 2014: 213–19.
8 See Dawson's essay, 'Performance and Participation' in Dawson and Yachnin 2001: 11–37, Yachnin's focus on spectacle in his 'Eye to Eye Opposed' (69–87), and Whitney 2006: 115–60.
9 Although apparently opposed to Weimann's strict demarcation of *locus* from *platea*, both Erika T. Lin and Mary Thomas Crane have implicitly recognized an instinctive line drawn between playworld and audience reality (see Lin 2012: especially 23–37; Crane 2001: 55–64).
10 Extensions of Weimann's original concepts into practical staging potential have been suggested by Erica Lin, in Lin 2006 and Wright 2017.
11 See Shell 2010: 175–222.

Conclusion

1 See also Auslander 2008: 107–19; Baugh 2005; Purcell 2014: 212–25. For some examples of extending the experience of spectating, see Sullivan 2018.

2 A fuller account of the philosophical underpinning of this position can be found in Bourne 2006.
3 For examples of how this might affect critical approaches, see Grady and Hawkes 2007, O'Rourke 2012.
4 This syndrome is further developed as a projection by the self in much recent psychoanalytic investigations; see Lawley and Tompkins 2000, especially 21–48.

REFERENCES

Abercrombie, N. and B. J. Longhurst (1998), *Audiences: A Sociological Theory of Performance and Imagination*, London: Sage.

Aebischer, P. (2017), 'Technology and the Ethics of Spectatorship', in J. C. Bulman (ed.), *The Oxford Handbook of Shakespeare and Performance*, 302–20, Oxford: Oxford University Press.

Altman, J. B. (1991), '"Vile Participation": The Amplification of Violence in the Theater of *Henry V*', *Shakespeare Quarterly*, 42: 1–32.

Anon. (1615), *New Characters*, 6th ed., London: printed by E. Griffin for L. Lisle.

Armstrong, P. B. (2000), 'The Politics of Play: The Social Implications of Iser's Literary Theory', *New Literary History*, 31: 211–23.

Auslander, P. (1999), *Liveness: Performance in a Mediatized Culture*, London: Routledge.

Auslander P. (2008), 'Live and Technologically Mediated Performance', in T. C. Davis (ed.), *The Cambridge Companion to Performance Studies*, 107–19, Cambridge: Cambridge University Press.

Austin, J. L. (1975), *How To Do Things With Words*, Cambridge, MA: Harvard University Press.

Bacon, F. (1640), *Of the advancement and proficence of learning; or, The partitions of sciences. Nine books written in Latin by the most eminent , illustrious, and famous Lord Francis Bacon Baron of Verulam Vicount of St Albans, Counsellor of Estate, and Lord Chancellor of England* . Oxford: printed by Leon Lichfield, for Robert Young and Edward Forrest.

Balme, C. B. (2014), *The Theatrical Pubic Sphere*, Cambridge: Cambridge University Press.

Bathurst, C. (1857), *Remarks on the Differences in Shakespeare's Versification in Different Periods of his Life and on the Like Points of Difference in Poetry Generally*, London: J. W. Parker.

Baugh, C. (2005), *Theatre, Performance, and Technology: The Development of Scenography in the 20th Century*, Basingstoke: Palgrave Macmillan.
de Beauvoir, S. (1949), *The Second Sex*, trans. H. M. Parshley, London: Everyman.
Bell, D. (1990), *Husserl*, London: Routledge.
Benjamin, W. (1968), *Illuminations: Essays and Reflections*, trans. Harry Zohn., ed. Hannah Arendt, New York: Schoken Books.
Bennett, S. ([1990] 1997), *Theatre Audiences*, 2nd ed., London: Routledge.
Bleich, D (1975), *Readings and Feelings: An Introduction to Subjective Criticism*, Urbana: National Council of Teachers of English.
Bleich, D. (1978), *Subjective Criticism*, Baltimore: Johns Hopkins University Press.
Bleich, D. (2004), 'What Literature is Ours?', in P. Schweickart (ed.), *Reading Sites: Social Difference and Reader Response*, 286–313, New York: Modern Language Association.
Bloom, H. (1998), *The Invention of the Human*, New York: Riverhead.
Bohman, J. (2004), 'Expanding Dialogue: The Internet, the Public Sphere and Prospects for Transnational Democracy' in N. Crossley and M. Roberts (eds), *After Habermas: New Perspectives on the Public Sphere*, 131–55, Oxford: Blackwell.
Bonnefoy, Y. (1990), 'Lifting Our Eyes from the Page', trans. J. Naughton, *Critical Inquiry*, 16: 794–806.
Bourne, C. (2007), *The Future of Presentism*, Oxford: The Clarendon Press.
Brook, P. (1968), *The Empty Space: A Book About the Theatre: Deadly, Holy, Rough, Immediate*, London: Penguin Books.
Brotton, J. (1998), '"This Tunis, sir, was Carthage": Colonialism in *The Tempest*', in A. Loomba and M. Orkin (eds), *Post-Colonial Shakespeares*, 23–42, London: Routledge.
Brown, C. (2015), *Shakespeare and Psychoanalytic Theory*, London: Bloomsbury Arden Shakespeare.
Brown, P. (1985), '"This thing of darkness I acknowledge mine": *The Tempest* and the Discourse of Colonialism', in J. Dollimore and A. Sinfield (eds), *Political Shakespeares*, 48–71, Manchester: Manchester University Press.
Bruster, D. (2000), 'The Structural Transformation of Print in Late Elizabethan England', in A. E. Marotti and M. D. Bristol (eds), *Print, Manuscript, Performance: The Changing Relations of the*

Media in Early Modern England, 49–89, Columbus: Ohio State University Press.

Bullough, G. (ed.) (1957–75), *Narrative and Dramatic Sources of Shakespeare*, 8 vols, London: Routledge and Kegan Paul.

Butler, J. ([1990] 1999), *Gender Trouble: Feminism and the Subversion of Identity*, anniversary ed., London: Routledge.

Butler, J. (2015), *Notes Toward a Performative Right to Assembly*, Cambridge, MA: Harvard University Press.

Calderwood, J. L. (1966), '*Coriolanus*: Wordless Meanings and Meaningless Words', *SEL*, 6: 211–24.

Cannon, C. K. (1971), '"As in a Theater": *Hamlet* in the Light of Calvin's Doctrine of Predestination', *Studies in English Literature*, 11: 203–22.

Césaire, A. ([1955] 1972), *Discourse on Colonialism*, trans. J. Pinkham, New York: Monthly Review Press.

Chambers, E. K. (1923), *The Elizabethan Stage*, 4 vols, Oxford: Oxford University Press.

Clegg, C. S. (2017), *Shakespeare's Reading Audiences: Early Modern Books and Audience Interpretation*, Cambridge: Cambridge University Press.

Cohen D. M. (1980), 'The Jew and Shylock', *Shakespeare Quarterly*, 31: 53–63.

Coleridge, S. T. (1960), *Shakespearean Criticism*, ed. T. M. Raysor, 2 vols, London: J. M. Dent.

Coleridge, S. T. (1983), *The Collected Works of Samuel Taylor Coleridge: Biographia Literaria*, ed. J. Engell and W. J. Bate, Princeton: Princeton University Press.

Cook, A. (2013), 'Texts and Embodied Performance', in N. Shaughnessy (ed.), *Affective Performance and Cognitive Science: Body, Brain and Being*, 83–90, London: Bloomsbury.

Cowan, J. L. (2016), 'The Imagination's Arts: Poetry and Natural Philosophy in Bacon and Shakespeare', *Studies in Philology*, 113: 132–62.

Crane, M. T. (2001), *Shakespeare's Brain: Reading with Cognitive Theory*, Princeton: Princeton University Press.

Crosse, H. (1603), *Vertues common-vvealth: or The high-way to honour Wherin is discouered, that although by the disguised craft of this age, vice and hypocrisie may be concealed: yet by tyme (the triall of truth) it is most plainly reuealed*. London: printed by T. Creede for I. Newbery.

Culler, J. (1975), *Structuralist Poetics: Structuralism, Linguistics and the Study of Literature*, London: Routledge and Kegan Paul.

Culler, J. (1981), *The Pursuit of Signs: Semiotics, Literature, Deconstruction*, London: Routledge and Kegan Paul.

Culler, J. (1983), *On Deconstruction: Theory and Criticism After Structuralism*, London: Routledge.

Cust, R. (2007), 'The "Public Man" in Late Tudor and Early Stuart England', in P. Lake and S. Pincus (eds), *The Politics of the Public Sphere in Early Modern England*, 16–43, Manchester: Manchester University Press.

Dasenbrock, R. W. (1986), 'Accounting for the Changing Certainties of Interpretive Communities', *Modern Language Notes*, 101: 1022–41.

Davies, Sir J. (1876), 'In Cosmum', 'Epigrammes 17', in Rev. A. Grosart (ed.), *The Complete Poems of Sir John Davies*, 2 vols, London: Chatto and Windus.

Dawson, A. and P. Yachnin (2001), *The Culture of Playgoing in Shakespeare's England: A Collaborative Debate*, Cambridge: Cambridge University Press.

de Man, P. (2001), 'Reading and History', in J. L. Machor and P. Goldstein (eds), *Reception Study: From Literary Theory to Cultural Studies*, 326–7, New York: Routledge.

Detmer, E. (1997), 'Civilizing Subordination: Domestic Violence and *The Taming of the Shrew*', *Shakespeare Quarterly*, 48: 273–94.

Dewey, J. (1934), *Art as Experience*, London: Penguin.

Dillon, J. (2000), *Theatre, Court and City, 1595–1610*, Cambridge: Cambridge University Press.

Dimock, W.-C. (1991), 'Feminism, New Historicism, and the Reader', *American Literature*, 63: 601–22.

Dolan, J. ([1991] 2012), *The Feminist Spectator as Critic*, 2nd ed., Ann Arbor: University of Michigan Press.

Doty, J. S. (2017), *Shakespeare, Popularity and the Public Sphere*, Cambridge: Cambridge University Press.

Doty, J. S. and M. Gurnis (2018), 'Theatre Scene and Theatre Public in Early Modern London', *Shakespeare*, 14: 12–25.

Downes, J. (1708), *Roscius Anglicanus, or, an historical review of the stage, After it had been Suppress'd by means of the late Unhappy Civil War, begun in 1641, 'till the Time of King Charles the IId's. Restoration, in May, 1660. Giving an Account of its Rise again; of the Time and Places the Governours of both the*

Companies first erected their Theatres. The Names of the Principal Actors and Actresses, who Performed in the Chiefest Plays in each House. With the Names of the most taking Plays, and Modern Poets, for the space of 46 Years, and during the Reign of Three Kings, and part of our present Sovereign Lady, Queen Anne, from 1660, to 1706, London: H. Playford.

Dustagheer, S. (2014), 'Experimentation in Shakespeare's London', in H. Crawforth, S. Dustagheer and J. Young (eds), *Shakespeare in London*, 213–19, Arden Shakespeare, London: Bloomsbury.

Eagleton, T. (1981), *Walter Benjamin, or Towards a Revolutionary Criticism*, London: Verso.

Eagleton, T. (2012), *The Event of Literature*, New Haven: Yale University Press.

Eco, U. (1977), 'Semiotics of Theatrical Performance', *Drama Review*, 21: 107–17.

Eco, U. (1979), *The Role of the Reader: Explorations in the Semiotics of Texts*, Bloomington: Indiana University Press.

Edwards, L. (1972), 'Women, Energy, and *Middlemarch*', *Massachusetts Review*, 13; 223–38.

Fanon, F. [1952] 1967), *Black Skin, White Masks*, trans. C. L. Markmann, London: Pluto Press.

Farabee, D. (2014), *Shakespeare's Staged Spaces and Playgoers' Perceptions*, Basingstoke: Palgrave Macmillan.

Felperin H. (1995), 'Political Criticism at the Crossroads', in N. Wood (ed.), The Tempest: *Theory in Practice*, 29–66, Buckingham and Bristol: Open University Press.

Fetterley, J. (1978), *The Resisting Reader: A Feminist Approach to American Fiction*, Bloomington: Indiana University Press.

Findlay, A. (2018), 'Shakespeare, Ceremony and the Public Sphere of Performance', *Shakespeare*, 14: 26–37.

Fish, S. (1967), *Surprised by Sin: The Reader in Paradise Lost*, Cambridge, MA: Harvard University Press.

Fish, S. (1970), 'Literature in the Reader: Affective Stylistics', *New Literary History*, 2: 123–62.

Fish, S. (1972), *Self-Consuming Artifacts: The Experience of Seventeenth-Century Literature*, Berkeley: University of California Press.

Fish, S. (1978), 'Normal Circumstances, Literal Language, Direct Speech Acts, the Ordinary, the Everyday, the Obvious, What Goes Without Saying, and Other Special Cases', *Critical Inquiry*, 4: 625–44.

Fish, S. (1980), *Is There a Text in This Class?: The Authority of Interpretive Communities*, Cambridge, MA: Harvard University Press.

Fish, S. (1981), 'Why No One's Afraid of Wolfgang Iser', *Diacritics*, 11: 2–13.

Fish, S. (1989), *Doing What Comes Naturally: Change, Rhetoric, and the Practice of Theory in Literary and Legal Studies*, Oxford: Clarendon Press.

Fluck, W. (2000), 'The Search for Distance: Negation and Negativity in Wolfgang Iser's Literary Theory', *New Literary History*, 31: 175–210.

Fraser, N. (2014), 'Transnationalizing the Public Sphere', in K. Nash (ed.), *Transnationalizing the Public Sphere*, 8–42, Cambridge: Polity Press.

Freud, S. (1999), *The Interpretation of Dreams*, trans. J. Crick, Oxford: Oxford University Press.

Freund, E. (1987), *The Return of the Reader: Reader-Response Criticism*, London: Methuen.

Frow, J. (1991), 'Tourism and the Semiotics of Nostalgia', *October*, 57: 123–51.

Frow, J. (2001), 'Economies of Value' in J. L. Machor and P. Goldstein (eds), *Reception Study: From Literary Theory to Cultural Studies*, 294–318, New York: Routledge.

Frye, N. (1957), *Anatomy of Criticism*, Princeton: Princeton University Press.

Fulbrook, M. (2002), *Historical Theory: Ways of Imagining the Past*, London: Routledge.

Gadamer, H.-G. (2014), *Truth and Method*, rev. trans. by J. Weinsheimer and D. G. Marshall, 2nd ed., London: Bloomsbury.

Gadamer, H.-G. (2019), *Hermeneutics between History and Philosophy: The Selected Writings of Hans-Georg Gadamer*, vol. 1, trans. P. Vandevelde and A. Iyer, London: Bloomsbury.

Gajowski, E. (ed.) (2009), *Presentism, Gender, and Sexuality in Shakespeare*, Basingstoke: Palgrave Macmillan.

Gibson J. J. (1979), *The Ecological Approach to Visual Perception*, Boston: Houghton Mifflin.

Gilman, E. B. (1980), '"All Eyes": Prospero's Inverted Masque', *Renaissance Quarterly*, 33: 214–30.

Gosson, S. (1579), *Schoole of Abuse: Containing a pleasant invective against Poets, Pipers, Players, Jesters and such-like Caterpillars of a commonwealth*, London: printed for T. Woodcocke.

Gosson, S. (1582), *Playes Confuted in Five Actions, Proving that they are not to be suffred in a Christian Common Wealthe*, London: imprinted for T. Gosson.

Gosson, S. (1598), *The Trumpet of Warre. A sermon preached at Paules Crosse the seuenth of Maie*, London: by V. S[immes] for I. O[xenbridge].

Grady, H. and T. Hawkes (eds) (2007), *Presentist Shakespeares*. London and New York: Routledge.

Grady, H. (2008), 'Shakespeare and Impure Aesthetics: The Case of *A Midsummer Night's Dream*', *Shakespeare Quarterly*, 59: 274–302.

Graff, G. G. (1985), 'Interpretation on Tiön: A Response to Stanley Fish', *New Literary History*, 17: 109–17.

Greenblatt S. (1988), 'Martial Law in the Land of Cockaigne', in *Shakespearean Negotiations: The Circulation of Social Energy in Renaissance England*, 129–63, Oxford: Clarendon Press.

Grotowski, J. with L. Flaszen (1968), *Towards a Poor Theatre*, ed. E. Barba, London: Methuen.

Gurr, A. ([1987] 1996), *Playgoing in Shakespeare's London*, 2nd ed., Cambridge: Cambridge University Press.

Gurr, A. ([1992] 2009), *The Shakespearean Stage, 1574–1642*, 4th ed., Cambridge: Cambridge University Press.

Habermas, J. ([1962] 1989), *The Structural Transformation of the Public Sphere: An Inquiry Into a Category of Bourgeois Society*, trans. T. Burger and F. Lawrence, Cambridge: MIT Press.

Habermas, J. (2018), 'Theory of Rationality and Theory of Meaning', in *Philosophical Investigations*, trans. C. Cronin, 79–99, Cambridge: Polity Press.

Hamer, M. (1996), 'Reading *Antony and Cleopatra* through Irigaray's *Speculum*', in N. Wood (ed.), *Antony and Cleopatra (Theory in Practice)*, 66–91, Buckingham and Philadelphia: Open University Press.

Hazlitt, W. ([1908] 2009), *Characters of Shakespeare's Plays*, ed. J. M. Lobban, rev. ed., Cambridge: Cambridge University Press.

Hirsch, E. D. (1967), *Validity of Interpretation*, New Haven: Yale University Press.

Hirsch, E .D. (1976), *The Aims of Interpretation*, Chicago: University of Chicago Press.
Hirsch, E .D. (1983), 'Past Intentions and Present Meanings', *Essays in Criticism*, 44: 79–98.
Hirsch, E. D. (1984), 'Meaning and Significance Reinterpreted', *Critical Inquiry*, 11: 202–25.
Hirschfeld, H. (2006), '"We All Expect a Gentle Answer, Jew": *The Merchant of Venice* and the Psychotheology of Conversion', *English Literary History*, 73: 61–81.
Holland, N. N. (1968), *The Dynamics of Literary Response*, Oxford: Oxford University Press.
Holland, N. N. (1975), *5 Readers Reading*, New Haven: Yale University Press.
Holland, N. N. (1980), 'Unity Identity Text Self', in J. P. Tompkins (ed.), *Reader-Response Criticism: From Formalism to Post-Structuralism*, 118–33, Baltimore: Johns Hopkins University Press.
Holland, N. N. (2009), *Literature and the Brain*, Gainesville: PsyArt Foundation.
Hosley, R. (1961), 'Was There a "Dramatic Epilogue" to *The Taming of the Shrew*?', *Studies in English Literature*, 1: 17–34.
Hosley, R. (1964), 'Sources and Analogues of *The Taming of the Shrew*', *Huntington Library Quarterly*, 27: 289–308.
Husserl, E. ([1939] 1973), *Experience and Judgement*, trans. J. Churchill and K. Ameriks, London: Routledge.
Husserl, E. ([1913] 1982), *Ideas Pertaining to a Pure Phenomenology and a Phenomenological Philosophy, General Introduction to a Pure Phenomenology*, vol. 1, trans. F. Kersten, The Hague: Nijhoff.
Husserl, E. (2006), *The Basic Problems of Phenomenology: From the Lectures, Winter Semester, 1910–11*, trans. I. Farin and J. G. Hart, Dordrecht: Springer Press.
Hutton V. (1985), '*A Midsummer Night's Dream*: Tragedy in Comic Disguise', *Studies in English Literature*, 25: 289–305.
Ingarden, R. (1973a), *The Literary Work of Art: An Investigation on the Borderlines of Ontology, Logic, and Theory of Literature*, trans. G. G. Grabowicz, Evanston: Northwestern University Press.
Ingarden, R. (1973b), *The Cognition of the Work of Art*, trans. R. A. Crowley and K. R. Olson, Evanston: Northwestern University Press.

Iser, W. (1978a), *The Act of Reading: A Theory of Aesthetic Response*, Baltimore: Johns Hopkins University Press.

Iser, W. ([1974] 1978b), *The Implied Reader: Patterns of Communication in Prose Fiction from Bunyan to Beckett*, Baltimore: Johns Hopkins University Press.

Iser, W. (1980), 'Interview: Wolfgang Iser' (with R. E. Kuenzli, N. Holland. W. C. Booth and S. Fish), *Diacritics*, 10: 57–74.

Iser, W. (1981), 'Talk Like Whales: A Reply to Stanley Fish', *Diacritics*, 11: 82–7.

Iser, W. (1984), 'The Interplay Between Creation and Interpretation', *New Literary History*, 15: 387–95.

Iser, W. (1993a), *The Fictive and the Imaginary: Charting Literary Anthropology*, Baltimore: Johns Hopkins University Press.

Iser, W. (1993b), *Prospecting: From Reader Response to Literary Anthropology*, Baltimore: Johns Hopkins University Press.

Iser, W. (1993c), *Staging Politics: The Lasting Impact of Shakespeare's Histories*, trans. D H. Wilson, New York: Columbia University Press.

Iser, W. (2000), *The Range of Interpretation*, New York: Columbia University Press.

Jauss, H. R. (1982a), 'Literary History as a Challenge to Literary Theory', in H. R. Jauss (ed.), *Toward an Aesthetic of Reception*, trans. T. Bahti, 3–45, Minneapolis: University of Minnesota Press.

Jauss, H. R. (1982b), *Aesthetic Experience and Literary Hermeneutics*, trans. M. Shaw, Minneapolis: University of Minnesota Press.

Jonson, B. (1609a), *The Masque of Queenes Celebrated from the House of Fame*, London: by N. Okes for R. Bonian and H. Wally.

Jonson, B. (1609b), *The Case is Alter'd*, London: B. Sutton and W. Barrenger.

Kahneman, D. (2011), *Thinking, Fast and Slow*, London: Penguin.

Katz, D. A. (2018), '*Theatrum Mundi*: Rhetoric, Romance, and Legitimation in *The Tempest* and *The Winter's Tale*', *Studies in Philology*, 115: 719–41.

Kaufman, P. I. (2006), 'English Calvinism and the Crowd: *Coriolanus* and the History of Religious Reform', *American Society of Church History*, 75: 314–42.

Kennedy, D. (2009), *The Spectator and the Spectacle: Audiences in Modernity and Postmodernity*, Cambridge: Cambridge University Press.

Kuhn, T. S. (1962), *The Structure of Scientific Revolutions*, Chicago: University of Chicago Press.
Kuzner, J. (2007), 'Unbuilding the City: Coriolanus and the Birth of Republican Rome', *Shakespeare Quarterly*, 58: 174–99.
Lake, P. (2007), 'The Politics of "Popularity" and the Public Sphere: The "Monarchical Republic" of Elizabeth I Defends Itself', in P. Lake and S. Pincus (eds), *The Politics of the Public Sphere in Early Modern England*, 59–94, Manchester: Manchester University Press.
Lakoff, G. and M. Johnson ([1980] 2003), *Metaphors We Live By*, Chicago: University of Chicago Press.
Lamb, M. (1980), *Antony and Cleopatra on the English Stage*, London: Associated University Presses.
Lawley, J. and P. Tompkins (2000), *Metaphors in Mind: Transformation through Symbolic Modelling*, New York: Developing Press.
Lefebvre, H. (1991), *The Production of Space*, trans. D. Nicholson-Smith, Oxford: Blackwell.
Lerer, S. (2018), *Shakespeare's Lyric Stage: Myth, Music, and Poetry in the Last Plays*, Chicago: University of Chicago Press.
Lin, E. T. (2006), 'Performance Practice and Theatrical Privilege: Rethinking Weimann's Concepts of Locus and Platea', *New Theatre Quarterly*, 22: 283–98.
Lin, E. T. (2012), *Shakespeare and the Materiality of Performance*, Basingstoke: Palgrave Macmillan.
Loomba, A. (1996), 'Shakespeare and Cultural Difference', in T. Hawkes (ed.), *Alternative Shakespeares*, vol. 2, 164–91, London: Routledge.
Mandel, J. (1973), 'Dream and Imagination in Shakespeare', *Shakespeare Quarterly*, 24: 61–8.
Mandler, J. M. (1984), *Stories, Scripts, and Scenes: Aspects of Schema Theory*, Hillsdale: Lawrence Erlbaum.
McConachie, B. (2006), 'Cognitive Studies and Epistemic Competence in Cultural History: Moving Theatre Studies beyond Freud and Lacan', in B. McConachie and F. E. Hart (eds), *Performance and Cognition: Theatre Studies and the Cognitive Turn*, 52–75, London: Routledge.
McConachie, B. (2008), *Engaging Audiences: A Cognitive Approach to Spectating in the Theatre*, Basingstoke: Palgrave Macmillan.

McConachie, B. (2013), 'Introduction: Spectating as Sandbox Play', in N. Shaughnessy (ed.), *Affective Performance and Cognitive Science: Body, Brain and Being*, 183–97, London: Bloomsbury.

McConachie, B. (2015), *Evolution, Cognition, Performance*, Cambridge: Cambridge University Press.

McLaughlin, L. (2004), 'Feminism and the Political Economy of Transnational Public Sphere', *Sociological Review*, 52: 156–75.

Merleau-Ponty, M. (2012), *Phenomenology of Perception*, trans. D. A. Landes, London: Routledge.

Metzger, M. J. (1998), '"Now by My Hood, a Gentle and No Jew": Jessica, *The Merchant of Venice*, and the Discourse of Early Modern English Identity', *PMLA*, 113: 52–63.

Mulcaster, R. (1975), 'The Quene's Majestie's Passage', in A. F. Kinney (ed.), *Elizabethan Backgrounds: Historical Documents of the Age of Elizabeth I*, Hamden: Archon.

Mullaney, S. (1988), *The Place of the Stage: License, Play, and Power in Renaissance England*, Ann Arbor: University of Michigan Press.

Müller-Doohm, S. ([2014] 2016), *Habermas: A Biography*, trans. D. Steuer, Cambridge: Polity Press.

Munday, A. (1590), *A Second and Third Blast of Retrait from Plaies and Theaters: the one whereof was sounded by a reuerend byshop dead long since; the other by a worshipful and zealous gentleman now aliue: one showing the filthines of plaies in times past; the other the abhomination of theaters in the time present: both expresly prouing that that common-weale is nigh vnto the cursse of God, wherein either plaiers be made of, or theaters maintained*, London: H. Denham.

Newman, K. (1987), 'Portia's Ring: Unruly Women and Structures of Exchange in *The Merchant of Venice*', *Shakespeare Quarterly*, 38: 19–33.

Ong, W. (1982), *Orality and Literacy: The Technologizing of the Word*, London: Methuen.

Orlin, L. C. (2015), 'Making Public the Private', in P. Yachnin and M. Eberhart (eds), *Forms of Association: Making Publics in Early Modern Europe*, 93–114, Amherst: University of Massachusetts Press.

O'Rourke, J. (2012), *Retheorizing Shakespeare Through Presentist Readings*, London and New York: Routledge.

Patterson, A. (1989), *Shakespeare and the Popular Voice*, Oxford: Basil Blackwell.
Platter, T. (1937), *Travels in England, 1599*, trans. C. Williams, London: Jonathan Cape.
Porter, L. (1995), 'Aimé Césaire's Reworking of Shakespeare: Anticolonialist Discourse in *Une Tempête*', *Comparative Literature Studies*, 32: 360–81.
Poulet, G. (1980), 'Criticism and the Experience of Interiority', in J. P. Tompkins (ed.), *Reader-Response Criticism: From Formalism to Post-Structuralism*, 41–9, Baltimore: Johns Hopkins University Press.
Purcell, S. (2013), *Shakespeare and Audience in Practice*, Basingstoke: Palgrave Macmillan.
Purcell S. (2014), 'The Impact of New Forms of Public Performance', in C. Carson and P. Kirwan (eds), *Shakespeare and the Digital World: Redefining Scholarship and Practice*, 212–25, Cambridge: Cambridge University Press.
Rabkin, N. (1977), 'Rabbits, Ducks, and *Henry V*', *Shakespeare Quarterly*, 28: 279–96.
Rancière, J. ([2008] 2009), *The Emancipated Spectator*, trans. G. Elliott, London: Verso.
Ray, W. (1984), *Literary Meaning: From Phenomenology to Deconstruction*, Oxford: Blackwell.
Rieff, P. (ed.) (1963), *Character and Culture: Psychoanalysis Applied to Anthropology, Mythology, Folklore, Literature and Culture in General*, New York: Collier.
Riss, A. (1992), 'The Belly Politic: *Coriolanus* and the Revolt of Language', *ELH*, 59: 53–75.
Rowlands, S. (1600), *The Letting of Humours Blood in the Head-Vaine*, London: W. White.
Rozett, M. T. (1985), 'The Comic Structures of Tragic Endings: The Suicide Scenes in *Romeo and Juliet* and *Antony and Cleopatra*', *Shakespeare Quarterly*, 36: 152–64.
Sartre, J.-P. ([1948] 2001), *What is Literature?*, trans. B. Frechtman, Abingdon: Routledge.
Sartre, J.-P. ([1940] 2004), *The Imaginary: A Phenomenological Psychology of the Imagination*, trans. J. Webbe, 2nd ed., London: Routledge.
Sartre, J.-P. ([2013] 2016), *What is Subjectivity?*, trans. D. Broder and T. Selous, London: Verso.

Schleiermacher, F. ([1838] 1990), *Hermeneutik und Kritik*, ed. M. Frank, Frankfurt: Suhrkamp.

Schweickart, P. (1986), 'Reading Ourselves: Toward a Feminist Theory of Reading', in P. Schweickart and E. Flynn (eds), *Gender and Reading: Essays on Readers, Texts, and Contexts*, 31–62, Baltimore: Johns Hopkins University Press.

Shakespeare, W. (1994a), *Coriolanus*, ed. R. B. Parker, Oxford: Oxford University Press.

Shakespeare, W. (1994b), *A Midsummer Night's Dream*, ed. P. Holland, Oxford: Oxford University Press.

Shakespeare, W. (1994c), *The Tempest*, ed. S. Orgel, Oxford: Oxford University Press.

Shakespeare, W. (1995), *Antony and Cleopatra*, ed. J. Wilders, Arden 3rd Series, London: Bloomsbury.

Shakespeare, W. (1996), *A Midsummer Night's Dream: Shakespeare in Production*, ed. T. Griffiths, Cambridge: Cambridge University Press.

Shakespeare, W. (1998), *Antony and Cleopatra: Shakespeare in Production*, ed. R. Madelaine, Cambridge: Cambridge University Press.

Shakespeare, W. (2000), *Coriolanus*, ed. L. Bliss, Cambridge: Cambridge University Press.

Shakespeare, W. (2010), *The Taming of the Shrew*, ed. B. Hodgdon, Arden 3rd Series, London: Bloomsbury.

Shakespeare, W. (2011), *The Arden Shakespeare Complete Works*, ed. R. Proudfoot, A. Thompson and D. S. Kastan, rev. ed., London: Arden Shakespeare.

Shakespeare, W. (2013), *Coriolanus*, ed. P. Holland, Arden 3rd Series, London: Bloomsbury.

Shapiro, J. (1996), *Shakespeare and the Jews*, New York: Columbia University Press.

Shell, A. (2010), *Shakespeare and Religion*, Arden Shakespeare, London: Bloomsbury.

Shrank C. (2003), 'Civility and the "City" in *Coriolanus*', *Shakespeare Quarterly*, 54: 406–23.

Sicher, E. S. (1991), 'The Jewing of Shylock: Wesker's *The Merchant*', *Modern Language Studies*, 21: 57–69.

Sidney, Sir P. (2002), *An Apology for Poetry (or The Defence of Poesy)*, ed. G. Shepherd, 3rd ed., rev. and expanded by R. W. Maslen, Manchester: Manchester University Press.

Simpson, J. (2019), *Permanent Revolution: The Reformation and the Illiberal Roots of Liberalism*, Cambridge, MA: Harvard University Press.
Smith, B. R. (1999), *The Acoustic World of Early Modern England*, Chicago: University of Chicago Press.
Smith, S. (2017), *Musical Response in the Early Modern Playhouse, 1603–1625*, Cambridge: Cambridge University Press.
Specter, M. G. (2010), *Habermas: An Intellectual Biography*, Cambridge: Cambridge University Press.
Stecker, R. (1990), 'Fish's Argument for the Relativity of Interpretive Truth', *Journal of Aesthetics and Art Criticism*, 48: 223–30.
Steggle, M. (2020), 'Title- and Scene-Boards: The Largest, Shortest Documents', in T. Stern (ed.), *Rethinking Theatrical Documents in Shakespeare's England*, 111–27, Arden Shakespeare, London: Bloomsbury.
Stern, T. (2004), *Making Shakespeare: From Page to Stage*, London: Routledge.
Stern T. (2009), *Documents of Performance in Early Modern England*, Cambridge: Cambridge University Press.
Styan, J. L. (1977), *The Shakespeare Revolution: Criticism and Performance in the Twentieth Century*, Cambridge: Cambridge University Press.
Sullivan, E. (2018), 'Shakespeare, Social Media and the Digital Public Sphere: *Such Tweet Sorrow* and *A Midsummer Night's Dreaming*', *Shakespeare*, 14: 64–79.
Sweeney, J. G. III (1985), *Jonson and the Psychology of Public Theater: To Coin the Spirit, Spend the Sou*, Princeton: Princeton University Press.
Thomas, B. (2008), '"The Fictive and the Imaginary: Charting Literary Anthropology": or, What's Literature Have to Do With It?', *American Literary History*, 20: 622–31.
Tiffany, G. (2003), '*Hamlet* and Protestant Aural Theater', *Christianity and Literature*, 52: 307–23.
Tompkins, J. P. (1978), 'Review of Bleich's *Subjective Criticism*', *Modern Language Notes*, 93: 1068–75.
Tompkins, J. P. (2001), 'Masterpiece Theater: The Politics of Hawthorne's Literary Reputation', in J. L. Machor and P. Goldstein (eds), *Reception Study: From Literary Theory to Cultural Studies*, 133–54, New York: Routledge.

Utterback, N. (2013), 'Embodied Memory and Extra-Daily Gesture', in N. Shaughnessy (ed.), *Affective Performance and Cognitive Science: Body, Brain and Being*, 147–58, London: Bloomsbury.

Vickers, B. (ed.) (1974–95), *William Shakespeare: The Critical Heritage*, 6 vols, London: Routledge.

Wagner, M. D. (2012), *Shakespeare, Theatre, and Time*, London: Routledge.

Weimann, R. (1978), *Shakespeare and the Popular Tradition in the Theater: Studies in the Social Dimension of Dramatic Form and Function*, ed. Robert Schwartz, Baltimore: Johns Hopkins University Press.

Weimann, R. (1992), 'Representation and Performance: The Uses of Authority in Shakespeare's Theatre', *PMLA*, 107: 497–510.

Weimann, R. (2000), *Author's Pen and Actor's Voice: Playing and Writing in Shakespeare's Theatre*, ed. H. Higbee and W. West, Cambridge: Cambridge University Press.

Whitney, C. (2006), *Early Responses to Renaissance Drama*, Cambridge: Cambridge University Press.

Wood, N. (2011), 'Civic Humanism: Said, Brecht and Coriolanus', in A. Mousley (ed.), *Towards a New Literary Humanism*, 212–27, Basingstoke: Palgrave Macmillan.

Wood, N. (2018), 'Introduction: Shakespeare's Public Spheres', *Shakespeare*, 14: 1–11.

Worthen, W. B. (1986), 'The Weight of Antony: Staging "Character" in *Antony and Cleopatra*', *Studies in English Literature*, 26: 295–308.

Worthen, W. B. (2017), 'Shakespearean Technicity', in J. Bulman (ed.), *The Oxford Handbook of Shakespeare and Performance*, 321–40, Oxford: Oxford University Press.

Wright, C. (2017), 'Ontologies of Play: Reconstructing the Relationship between Audience and Act in Early Modern Drama', *Shakespeare Bulletin*, 35: 187–206.

Zahavi, D. (2015), 'Phenomenology of Reflection', in *Commentary on Husserl's 'Ideas I'*, ed. A. Staithi, 177–94, Berlin: de Gruyter.

INDEX

Abercrombie, Nicholas 143
Aebischer, Pascale 152–3
aesthesis (Jauss) 40
aesthetic
  experience (Gadamer)
    17–18, 85
  knowledge (Jauss) 34–6,
    39
aesthetics
  of reading (Iser) 45–6
  of reception (Jauss) 36–8
affordances (McConachie)
  26–7, 166 n.10
Alexander, Bill 82, 102, 103
All For Love (Dryden) 33, 35
Altman, Joel B. 141–2
Antony and Cleopatra 8, 29–62,
  156
Apollonius of Tyre 136
Aristotle 47
Armstrong, Paul B. 167 n.7
As You Like It 10, 50, 148,
  152
Audibert, Justin 98
Auslander, Philip 143, 172 n.1
Austin, J.L. 11–12

Bacon, Francis 128–9
Balme, Christopher B. 9,
  171 n.2
Bathurst, Charles 35–6
Baugh, Christopher 172 n.1
Beckett, Samuel 152

being-in-the-world (Gadamer)
  16–17
Bell, David 165 n.1
Benjamin, Walter 156–7
Bennett, Susan 28–9
Benson, Frank 36
Bleich, David 8, 65, 68, 70–2,
  73, 78–9, 81, 83, 115–16,
  168, nn.8, 11
Bliss, Lee 169 n.7
Bloom, Harold 109–10, 113
Blythe, Dominic 100
Bohman, James 131
Bonnefoy, Yves 98–9, 103
Booth, Wayne C. 61
Bourne, Craig 172 n.2
Boyd, Michael 43
Branagh, Kenneth 141
Brecht, Bertolt 104–7, 112–13
Brewster, Yvonne 43
Brook, Peter 41–2, 81, 152
Brookes, Scarlett 102
Brotton, Jerry 170 n.16
Brown, Carolyn E. 25, 166 n.7
Brown, Paul 170 n.15
Bruster, Douglas 171 n.3
Bullough, Geoffrey 30, 101–2,
  167 n.2, 169 n.5
Butler, Judith 96
Byrne, Anthony 44

Caird, John 82–3, 100
Cake, Jonathan 43

Calderwood, James L. 108–9
Capell, Edward 33
catharsis (Jauss) 40
central fantasy (Holland) 69
Césaire, Aimé 97–8, 117
Chambers, E.K. 128
Clay, Caroline 100
Clegg, Cyndia Susan 171 n.3
Cleopatra and Antony 42–3
closed text (Eco) 51, 121
cognitive perception (Gadamer) 17–18
Cohen, Derek M. 169 n.3
Coleridge, Samuel Taylor 35, 114, 170 n.13
concretization
  (Ingarden) 20–1
  (Iser) 46
constative statements (Austin) 11–12
content fallacy (Holland) 27–8
Cook, Amy 25, 166 n.8
Coriolanus 8, 92, 104–9, 120, 129
Corrigan, James 102
Cowan, Jacqueline L. 167 n.1
Crane, Mary Thomas 28, 166 n.9, 171 n.9
critical play (Gadamer) 18
Crosse, Henry 127
Crotty, Derbhle 99–100
Culler, Jonathan 8, 73, 76–9, 83, 84–5, 86, 168, nn.9, 10
Cust, Richard 125

Daniel, Samuel 52
Daniels, Ron 82, 141
Dasenbrock, Reed Way 169 n.12
Davenant, William 116

Davies, Sir John 127
Dawson, Anthony 126, 134, 171 n.8
De Beauvoir, Simone 96
De Man, Paul 55
deconstruction 77–8
Detmer, Emily 170 n.11
Dewey, John 155–6
diffused audience (Abercrombie and Longhurst) 143
Dillon, Janette 171 n.7
Dimock, Wai-Chee 171 n.18
Disney, Walt 68
Dolan, Jill 98
Doran, Greg 98
Dorn, Franchelle 42
Doty, Jeffrey S. 9 , 125, 136
doubling of meaning (Iser) 50–1, 57
Downes, John 116–17
Dryden, John 33, 35, 43, 116
D'Silva, Darell 43
Dustagheer, Sarah 171 n.7

Eagleton, Terry 55, 120–1
Eco, Umberto 8, 10, 51–2
Edwards, Lee 95
Edwards, Malcolm 43
Elizabeth I 125
epistemic competence (McConachie) 26
Essex, Earl of 138

Famous Victories of Henry V, The 139
Fanon, Frantz 94–5
Farabee, Darlene 136
Felperin, Howard 170 n.15
Fetterley, Judith 8–9, 95–6, 120
Findlay, Alison 153

Findlay, Polly 102–3
Fiorentino, Ser Giovanni 101
Fish, Stanley 8, 58–61, 73–6,
    79–80, 83, 84, 86–7,
    167 n.6
Flaszen, Ludwig 152
Flaubert, Gustave 76
Fluck, Winifried 167 n.7
Fraser, Nancy 131
Freud, Sigmund 26, 64–5, 71–2,
    166 n.7, 168 n.8
Freund, Elizabeth 78, 168 n.11
Frow, John 9, 156
Frye, Northrop 65–6, 167–8 n.2
Fullbrook, Mary 26
functional code (Iser) 49

Gadamer, Hans-Georg 16–18,
    165 n.3
Gajowski, Evelyn 157
Garnier, Robert 52
Garrick, David 33
Gascoigne, George 111
Gibson, James J. 166 n.10
Gilman, E.B. 120
Glen, Iain 141
Goold, Rupert 97
Gosson, Stephen 126–8
Gower, John 136–7
Grady, Hugh 168 n.5
Graff, Gerald 169 n.13
Granville-Barker, Harley
    80–1
green world (Frye) 82,
    167–8 n.2
Greenblatt, Stephen 132,
    170 n.15
Griffiths, Trevor R. 80
Grotowski, Jerzy 152
Gurnis, Missa 125

Gurr, Andrew 133–4, 171 n.7
Gwilym, Mike 82

Habermas, Jürgen 9, 123–5,
    130–1, 135–6, 171 n.1
Haigh, Kenneth 42
Hall, Edward 50
Hamer, Mary 167 n.5
Hamlet 9–10, 12, 21, 24, 142–6
having-to-be (Sartre) 22
Hawkes, Terence 172 n.3
Hawthorne, Nathaniel 9
Hazlitt, William 35
Helpmann, Robert 41
Henry IV, Part 1 3–4, 139
Henry IV, Part 2 51, 139
Henry V 9–10, 126, 132,
    136–42
Henry VI, Parts 1–3 138
Henry, Susan 43
Hinman, Charlton 59
Hirsch, E.D. 113–15, 170 n.14
Hirschfeld, Heather 169 n.2
Hodgdon, Barbara 112, 170,
    n.10, 12
Holinshed, Raphael 50
Holland, Norman 8, 10, 27–8,
    61–2, 65, 68–70, 73,
    78–9, 81, 83, 168 n.6
Holland, Peter 108, 109,
    168 n.4
horizon (Gadamer) 19
horizon of expectations (Jauss)
    32–4, 37–8, 42, 44–5,
    54–5
horizon-consciousness (Husserl)
    15–16
Hosley, Richard 170 n.12
Hounsu, Djimon 98
Howard, Alan 42

Hunter, Kathryn 43
Husserl, Edmund 14–16, 165 n.2
Hutton, Virgil 168 n.5

ideal reader (Iser) 54, 84–5
identity themes (Holland) 10, 73–4
imaginary (Sartre) 23, 48
immasculation (Fetterley) 95
implied reader (Iser) 45–7, 55
Ingarden, Roman 16, 19–21, 27, 165 n.4
intentional object (Husserl) 16
interpretive
    code (Iser) 49
    community (Fish) 25, 73–6
    creation (Iser) 62
irreality (Sartre) 24
Iser, Wolfgang 8, 42–58, 68, 91–2, 114, 167 n.6

Jackson, Glenda 42
Jacobs, Sally 81
James I 107, 108–9
Jauss, Hans Robert 7, 32–44, 68
Johnson, Mark 157–8
Johnson, Richard 41
Johnson, Samuel 35
Jonson, Ben 127–8, 129, 171 n.4
Joyce, James 45
Julia, Raul 121
Juliani, John 97
Julius Caesar 128, 129, 156

Kahn, Michael 42
Kahneman, Daniel 158–60
Kalukango, Joaquina 43, 167 n.4

Katz, David A. 148
Kaufman, Peter Iver 148
Kean, Charles 80, 141
Kemble, Charles 33
Kennedy, Dennis 143–4, 170 n.16
Khan, Iqbal 44
King Lear 26, 49–50, 146, 152
Kuenzli, Rudolf E. 61
Kuhn, T.S. 70, 168 n.7
Kuzner, James 170 n.9

Lacan, Jacques 26
Lacy, James 117
Lake, Peter 124–5
Lakoff, George 157–8
Lamb, Margaret 30
Lamos, Mark 100
Laurier, Angela 81–2
Lawley, James D. 172 n.4
Lawrence, Josie 121
Lefebvre, Henri 131–2
Leiren-Young, Mark 97
Lepage, Robert 81
Lerer, Seth 119
life-world (Husserl) 15
Lin, Erika T. 28, 171, n.9, 10
literary competence (Culler) 25, 76–8, 84
Longhurst, Brian J. 143
Loomba, Ania 170 n.16

McAnuff, Des 5
Macbeth 10, 15–16, 49–50
McConachie, Bruce 26–7, 166 n.10, 166 n.11
McCowen, Alec 118
McCraney, Tarell Alvin 43
McLaughlin, Lisa 131
McMillan, Kenneth 3

Macready, William Charles 33, 141
McTeer, Janet 82
Madelaine, Richard 34, 41, 166 n.1
Mandel, Jerome 167 n.1
Mandler, Jean 166 n.9
mass audience (Abercrombie and Longhurst) 143
Mendelssohn, Felix 80, 83
Mendes, Sam 118
Merchant, The (Wesker) 97
Merchant of Vegas, The 97
Merchant of Venice, The 8, 9, 32, 92, 97–104, 120, 121
Merleau-Ponty, Maurice 73
method (Gadamer) 16–17
Metzger, Mary Janell 169 n.2
Michell, Keith 41
Middleton, Thomas 110
Midsummer Night's Dream, A 8, 10, 24, 63–89, 112, 132, 156
Mirren, Helen 98
Mulcaster, Richard 132
Mullaney, Steven 171 n.7
Müller-Doohm, Stefan 171, 5
Munday, Anthony 147–8

Nashe, Thomas 129
Newman, Karen 101
Noble, Adrian 1, 41–2
North, Sir Thomas 36–7, 56, 107
not-knowing (Sartre) 22
Nunn, Trevor 41, 100, 103

Olivier, Laurence 141
Omambala, Chu 100
Ong, Walter J. 11
open text (Eco) 52

Orgel, Stephen 120
Orlin, Lena Cowen 130
O'Rourke, James 172 n.3
Othello 42, 110

paradigm community (Fullbrook) 26
Parker, R.B. 107, 170 n.9
Parsons, Estelle 42
Patterson, Annabel 138
Pembroke, Countess of 52
pensiveness (Rancière) 94, 100–1, 108–9, 161
performative statements (Austin) 11–12
Pericles 136–7
Peter, John 118
Platter, Thomas 128
play
    Gadamer 18, 27
    Iser 48–9
Pleasant Conceited Historie, called The taming of a Shrew, A 111–12
Plutarch 30–1, 36–7, 43, 52, 56, 107, 167 n.2
Poel, William 81
poiesis (Jauss) 40
Porter, Laurence 97
Poulet, Georges 165–6 n.6
presentism 156–7
Pryce, Jonathan 42
public sphere (Habermas) 9–10, 123–5, 135–6
Purcell, Stephen 153, 172 n.1

Quayle, John 1

Rabkin, Norman 142
Rackham, Arthur 68

Rancière, Jacques 93–4, 100–1, 108–9, 161
Ray, William 83–4, 113, 168 n.11
Reinhardt, Max 81
resymbolization (Bleich) 71–3, 83
Richard II 171 n.3
Richard III 129
Richardson, Tony 41
Riss, Arthur 170 n.8
Romeo and Juliet 98
Rowe, Nicholas 33
Rowlands, Samuel 127
Rozett, Martha Tuck 166–7 n.1
Russell, Sophie 43
Russell-Beale, Simon 118
Rutherford, Malcolm 118
Rylance, Mark 167 n.3

Sartre, Jean-Paul 21–2, 48, 165, n.5
Schleiermacher, Friedrich 91–2
Scholes, Robert 86
Schweickart, Patrocinio 96
secondary revision of dreams (Freud) 64–5
Sedley, Sir Charles 33, 35
Sejanus 171 n.4
Sekacz, Ilona 83
Serreau, Jean-Marie 97
Shadwell, Thomas 117
Shapiro, James 169 n.2
Sheen, Michael 141
Shell, Alison 172 n.11
Shrank, Cathy 169 n.7
Siberry, Michael 121
Sicher, Efraim 169 n.1
side text (Ingarden) 20–1
Simon, Josette 44, 100

Simpson, James 147
Smith, Bruce R. 171 n.17
Smith, Simon 171 n.17
Specter, Matthew G. 171 n.5
Spencer, Charles 167 n.4
Stecker, Robert 169 n.12
Steggle, Matthew 171 n.2
Stern, Tiffany 171, n.2, 6
Sterne, Laurence 45
Stevenson, Juliet 82
Stewart, Patrick 42
Streep, Meryl 121
structural code (Iser) 49
structuralism 76–7
Styan, J.L. 152
Sullivan, Erin 172 n.1
Supposes (Gascoigne) 111
Suzman, Janet 41
Sweeney, John Gordon 171 n.4

Taming of the Shrew, The 8, 32, 92, 98, 110–13, 120, 121
Tempest, The 8, 9, 28, 92, 97–8, 116–20, 132
Thacker, David 99
Thomas, Brook 167 n.7
Tiffany, Grace 147
Timon of Athens 148, 156
Titus Andronicus 42
Tomelty, Frances 100
Tompkins, Jane 9, 168 n.11
Tompkins, Penny L. 172 n.4
Tree, Herbert Beerbohm 36, 80
Troilus and Cressida 1, 98
Twelfth Night 1–2, 4, 10, 26, 132, 152
Twine, Lawrence 137
Two Gentlemen of Verona, The 132

Utterback, Neal 166 n.8

Vickers, Brian 35
Vorfindlichkeiten (Husserl) 14

Wagner, Matthew D. 135
Warchus, Matthew 141
Wardle, Irving 118
Webster, John 129
Weimann, Robert 134–5
Wesker, Arnold 97–8, 169 n.1
Whiting, Margaret 41
Whitney, Charles 171 n.8

Whyman, Erica 98
Wilde, Patrick 43
Wilkins, George 137
Women Beware Women
 (Middleton) 110
Wood, Nigel 155, 169 n.7
Worthen, W.B. 153, 166 n.1
Wright, Clare 171 n.10

Yachnin, Paul 126, 134, 171 n.8

Zahavi, Dan 165 n.1
Zohn, Harry 157

www.ingramcontent.com/pod-product-compliance
Lightning Source LLC
Chambersburg PA
CBHW070636300426
44111CB00013B/2135